I. INTRODUCTION

In highly competitive markets characterized by low consumer search costs, we would expect product price and product quality to be strongly and positively correlated. If consumers can search easily among competitors and readily assess price and quality, those sellers providing higher quality will be able to charge a higher price to willing customers. Those failing to provide quality commensurate with price will lose customers and be forced to lower their price or exit the market.

If, however, consumers must incur significant costs to obtain accurate price and/or quality information, a high correlation between these two product attributes need not exist in equilibrium.[1] Presumably, the higher are search costs, the less likely consumers will be able to recognize good buys and bad buys before purchase, and the lower will be the correlation between price and quality. In the extreme case where consumers have no ability whatsoever to discern variations in quality pre-purchase, and assume simply that all products are of "average" quality, a variant of Gresham's Law will in sequential fashion drive higher quality providers from the market, since they will not be able to charge a sufficient premium to cover their greater production costs. Average quality will continue to decline until the products left in the market are of equally low quality. Although there would be a perfect correlation between price and quality at this degenerative point, this perfect correlation would signify a complete market failure [1].

A. Prior Research on Price-Quality Correlations

The degree of correlation between product price and quality in U.S. product markets has been explored extensively in a literature that dates back to 1950 [12]. The basic methodology of these studies is remarkably uniform. Product quality ratings usually are based on tests conducted by Consumer Reports ("CR").[2] The authors then calculate a correlation coefficient for these quality rankings and the list prices or, when available, the actual transaction prices for the tested

---

[1] The first theoretical treatment of price dispersion as an indicator of market imperfection appears in Stigler [16]. Stigler treated the initial existence of price dispersion as exogenous, and employed a simple consumer search model to explain why this condition would persist. Later treatments have attempted to explain the initial variation in prices. Usually, it is assumed that consumers differ in the amount of search they are willing to undertake, and that sellers specialize in serving either high or low-search consumers. Some sellers might, for example, bid for a particularly convenient location and charge a higher price to consumers who do not wish to search for a lower price. Other sellers with less advantageous sites will specialize in charging lower prices to consumers who are willing to search extensively to find the best deal. Entry will equalize the marginal return to the different strategies, and price dispersion will persist in equilibrium [4].

[2] A few of these studies use results from Consumers Research, and one article employed rankings of running shoes published in Runners World [2].

products. The results of these studies have also been quite consistent. In general, price and quality are only weakly correlated, with coefficients usually ranging from .20 to .25 [7]. These results are construed as evidence that consumer product markets perform "poorly," with one set of coauthors feeling motivated to title their article "The Chaos of Competition." [10]

This literature suffers from several weaknesses and limitations. Most obviously, the results can be no more reliable than CR's product ratings. Even if it is assumed that all of the CR protocols were appropriate and the tests performed competently, CR might not weight the various performance attributes for complex products such as stereo equipment, dishwashers, or tires in the same manner as would the average consumer.

And, if CR did happen to replicate the tastes of average consumers, significant subsets of buyers might still rank the products differently and willingly pay more for specialized products that might do relatively poorly in the ratings. Further, CR's ratings are not based on aesthetic qualities that may be very important to many consumers and that tend to be directly related to price.

Finally, sole reliance on CR automatically excludes all of the consumer service and retail industries that are supplied locally. Published studies of price and quality correlations for local services are limited to analyses of the legal and optometrical markets, where price advertising has been severely constrained [3]. We therefore have no systematic examinations of price and quality relationships in a major sector of the U.S. economy.

B. Current Research

The research reported in this working paper attempts to expand the limited scope and remedy some of the methodological weaknesses of prior studies of price-quality relationships in consumer industries. This analysis is made possible by the availability of an extensive data source for price and quality information for a large number of consumer service industries in the Washington, D.C. area. Such information has been published regularly by Washington Consumers' Checkbook since 1976.

Washington Consumers' Checkbook ("WCC") relies on quality evaluations supplied in response to mail questionnaires sent to all subscribers of Consumer Reports or WCC in the Washington area. Respondents are asked to rate service providers they have patronized during the last year as "superior," "adequate" or "inferior" on a variety of performance dimensions, such as "doing service properly," "starting and completing service promptly," and "overall performance." WCC "check rates" the firms that receive particularly high overall satisfaction ratings. Also reported is the number of consumers who rated each service provider.

The quality ratings are almost always accompanied by price information, usually in the form of an index. WCC staff contact each of the rated providers and ask for quotes on three or four standardized jobs. The providers' hourly labor rates are also listed where appropriate.

Although some establishments refuse to participate in this phase of WCC's research, ratings generally are available for 85-90 percent of the rated firms. WCC confers a check rating for price to the firms with the lowest price index scores.

In addition to price data, WCC customarily contacts local consumer protection offices to determine the number of complaints on file for each of the surveyed firms. (As discussed below, the complaint data provide one means of checking the reliability of the WCC survey results.) Finally, for approximately one-third of the rated industries, WCC gathers information from firms on the number of principal employees, such as auto mechanics or licensed plumbers. This information is used to normalize the complaint data for size of firm, and is not published separately.[3] WCC agreed, however, to provide all available employee data for the most recent rating period. These data serve as a measure of firm size in the statistical analysis.[4]

WCC Magazine is published on a roughly biannual basis, with approximately five or six industries per issue. For certain industries, such as medical professionals and financial institutions, WCC does not provide overall quality ratings and/or price index information. For the current research, suitably complete data were available for 19 service industries. In most cases, each industry was rated on several occasions over time. These industries are presented in Table I below, with the number of individual data sets for each industry given in parentheses.

---

[3] Assuming a firm has at least one complaint on file, the employee data can be derived using the absolute number of complaints and the complaint rate index, both of which are provided in the ratings. The majority of firms, however, have no complaints, thus precluding any indirect calculation of employee size.

[4] The ratings already contain a very rough indicator of firm size as measured by the number of respondents rating the various providers. These numbers will, however, be heavily skewed toward providers who have received high ratings in past issues of WCC, since respondents to the WCC questionnaire will be far more likely than the general public to have relied on those prior ratings as a shopping tool.

TABLE I
Local Service Industries in Sample

1. Air Conditioning-Heating Repair (5)	11. Locksmiths (3)
2. Auto Body Repair (5)	12. Pest Control (4)
3. Auto Mechanical Repair (8)	13. Plumbers (4)
4. Major Appliance Repair (4)	14. Restaurants (2)
5. Carpet Cleaning (3)	15. Shoe Repair (2)
6. Carpet Sales, Installation (2)	16. Supermarkets (3)
7. Computer Repair (3)	17. Tree Surgeons (1)
8. Drycleaning (2)	18. TV Repair (1)
9. Electricians (2)	19. Watch Repair (3)
10. Local Movers (3)	

WCC's approach to quality rankings avoids the major shortcoming of the Consumer Reports methodology. Since WCC quality ratings are based on actual consumer experience, they automatically reflect the weights that consumers assign to the various dimensions of firm performance. Although in some cases consumers may not be able to evaluate certain aspects of a service provider's competence and honesty as accurately as a trained tester, those ratings might still capture marked *differences* in quality among providers.

There is, however, a potentially high price to be paid for the consumer experience approach to rating service providers. The WCC "quality" ratings are really consumer "satisfaction" ratings. The ratings essentially measure how happy a consumer is after the service is completed and the bill is received. The difficulty is that the size of the bill may well influence the level of consumer satisfaction. Post purchase, most consumers will form a better opinion of, say, an auto repair establishment that presents a bill for $150 than with one that charges $450, even if there is no real difference in service quality.

This potential for bias exists irrespective of whether consumers have any clear knowledge of what competitors would have charged for the same job (although the magnitude of the bias would certainly be greater if patrons of the $450 shop were aware that they had paid a $300 premium). Higher bills inflict more pain, and the unfortunate recipients are less likely to reward providers with high ratings. Thus, depending on the strength of the bias, the WCC ratings could in theory reveal an inverse relationship between price and satisfaction even when the underlying relationship between price and true quality was positive.

Pre-purchase selection bias problems may also affect the satisfaction ratings. Consumers who choose to patronize higher cost establishments may also have higher expectations (and perhaps more complex service problems), and may therefore judge performance more critically, or be more likely to experience difficulties because of the nature of their particular service requests. Again, this potential bias in the WCC data may weaken or even reverse any positive relationship between price and quality that may actually exist in the surveyed service markets.

The price data published by WCC have their own potential problems. It would not be practical or prudent for WCC to gather price information as part of its consumer satisfaction survey. Even if consumers could remember price information reliably, there would in most instances be no way to pin down the precise nature and scope of the service that was provided. Thus, WCC gathers its own information, and is usually limited by time and budget constraints to soliciting price quotes for a small subset of the wide range of jobs provided by firms in most service industries. As a result, the price index based on these quotes is reliable only to the extent that the sampled prices reflect the prices of the services that consumers actually choose from each provider. As indicated earlier, WCC often publishes hourly labor data to supplement the price index, which provides a rough consistency check for the analysis.

The above difficulties not withstanding, the WCC ratings provide the most comprehensive source of information on price and quality in the local service sector that we are likely to have in the foreseeable future. It would not be economically feasible for a private tester such as Consumers Union to purchase such services directly and evaluate quality. There are simply too many providers and the cost of many of the services is too high. Further, unlike many of the durables tested by CR, services cannot be resold in the used market. The WCC data therefore deserve attention by researchers.

II. HYPOTHESES TESTED

A truly rigorous exploration of this subject area would begin with a complete structural model that would predict the equilibrium correlation between price and quality for firms in a given service industry based on production cost variables, consumer demand functions, and the magnitude of consumer search costs. Such a construct would allow us to test specific hypotheses concerning the absolute value of the correlation coefficient that we should expect in each of the the sample industries.

This study does not provide such a sophisticated underpinning, both due to the heroic scale of the theoretical challenges, and because suitable data would almost certainly not be available for many of the supply and demand variables that would be involved. Absent this theoretical construct, there is really very little we can say about the absolute correlations we would expect to see in these industries.

Presumably, none of the service industries included in this study fits the perfectly competitive model, if only because consumers must incur some search costs to determine firm price and quality. And, in any event, we would not expect even a highly efficient market to function perfectly at any and every moment in time. Snapshot measurements such as those relied upon here would always find instances of poor performance that had not yet been punished by the market. Finally, there are almost certainly measurement errors and other problems in the WCC price and quality data that could inject random noise and prevent precise measurement of the actual level of price-quality correlation in the market.[5]

At the other extreme, it is unlikely that any of the surveyed markets are completely "imperfect" in the sense that consumers are totally incapable of gathering any price or quality information whatever. Thus, about all we can predict about the absolute correlation between price and quality that we might observe from the WCC data for any given industry is that it should be greater than zero and less than one.[6]

Fortunately, the WCC data and existing theories from the literature on the economics of information allow us to test other interesting hypotheses concerning the expected comparative strength of price-quality correlations across service industries, and to test the accuracy of certain non-price "signals" that consumers might use to assess the quality of individual providers within industries. The availability of time series data for most of the sampled industries also permits an analysis of the stability of a firm's price and quality ratings over time. Specifically, it is possible to test whether a firm that receives a high rating for quality in an initial period is likely to "milk" any reputation gains and lower quality or raise its price in subsequent periods.

A. Price-Quality Correlations Across Industries

The first area for exploration is the pattern of price-quality correlations that we observe from industry to industry. Theory would predict that these correlations will be highest in those service markets where consumers can compare the prices and quality of competitors at low cost. It is relatively easy to specify the characteristics of a service that would determine how costly it would be for consumers to shop for price. Search will be easiest when the desired service is standardized, or comprised of standardized subcomponents, and the full scope of the needed service is known to the consumer before purchase. These characteristics would allow the consumer to gather price information efficiently by word-of-mouth, telephone, advertisements, or

---

[5] We will ignore for purposes of this discussion the possibly perverse bias introduced by any interaction between prices and consumer satisfaction that could reveal a seemingly negative price-quality correlation.

[6] Indeed, we would not necessarily expect a simple correlation of one in a perfectly functioning market. Although quality should increase monotonically with price under such circumstances, the relationship would not be linear unless the long run marginal cost of producing additional quality happened to be perfectly linear.

on-site inspection. The clearest examples of such services would be drycleaning, carpet cleaning, restaurants, and supermarkets.

Almost by definition, consumers cannot directly determine a service provider's quality until after the service is rendered. Still, there may be wide variance among industries in the ease with which quality can be evaluated post-purchase. In certain cases, quality can be evaluated fully by simple inspection or immediate experience. Again, restaurants, carpet cleaning, and drycleaning score well in this regard. In such instances, the quality reputation of firms would spread fairly quickly and allow new consumers to locate the desired combination of price and quality at minimal cost.

At the other end of the spectrum, comparative price and quality comparisons will be most difficult where the service is complex and the consumer may not know pre-purchase precisely which service components will be needed, or post-purchase whether the service had been fully or honestly rendered. Examples would include certain repair services for automobiles, appliances, and electronic entertainment items. The full cost of the repair would not be known until the provider had diagnosed the problem, at which point the consumer may already have incurred substantial out-of-pocket expenses and might be reluctant to repeat the process with another establishment.[7] Although consumers could determine post-purchase whether a repair had fixed the problem, they might not know whether all of the billed services were necessary.

Though not strictly a determinant of search cost, another factor bearing on price-quality correlation should be the relative frequency with which consumers purchase a given service. Clearly, consumers will have more opportunity to sample and compare competitors' offerings the more often they shop. For local services, this means (all else equal) that the market should punish poorly performing drycleaners more quickly than roofers who offer poor quality for the money. Although it was hoped that relative frequency of purchase could be quantified using existing marketing data or information supplied by the principal trade associations for each sampled industry, such data apparently are not available. Thus, very broad and subjective assessments of this and other consumer search costs factors are used to test whether price-quality correlations are in fact higher in low-search-cost industries.

B. Price-Quality Relationships Within Industries

The preceding analysis has focused on informational and purchase pattern considerations that might explain differing degrees of price-quality correlation across local service industries. It

---

[7] Comparative shopping will also be difficult or impractical when service is required on an emergency basis. There are many examples of service industries that may respond to emergency situations (e.g. Plumbers, Roofers, Air Conditioning and Heating firms, Auto Repair, and, for entertainment-challenged families, TV Repair), but this would not be the exclusive or even primary form of business for such firms. It is therefore difficult to sort industries on this basis.

would also be of interest to test theories that might predict which types of firms *within* a given industry are likely to offer higher levels of quality, or perhaps higher levels of value. That is, in those markets where consumers do not believe they can rely upon price as an accurate indicator of firm quality, are there other firm characteristics or practices that consumers can use as a time and money-saving substitute for extensive search in determining the level of quality and price that a firm is likely to provide?

1. Signaling Mechanisms

This issue has been treated extensively in the "signaling" literature, which originated in 1974 with Spence [15] and Nelson [11]. All else equal, it is hypothesized that higher quality providers will have a greater incentive to signal their advantage through advertising and through other bonding devices such as nontransferable physical capital (e.g., specialized building designs and accoutrements), the value of which is lost if consumers are disillusioned with a provider's quality post-purchase [8, 9]. In such cases, the advertising or other signal need not have any informational content *per se.* It is the mere existence and size of the advertising or other nontransferable physical investment that assures consumers that the firm is trustworthy and prepared to please customers over the long term.[8]

In some respects, service industries do not appear to fit the signaling model very well. First, with the exception of national chains and dealer franchises present primarily in the auto repair industry (discussed separately below), few of the firms in the industries rated by WCC engage in broadcast or other major media advertising. Many of the firms serve smaller regional markets and do not operate at a scale that would justify significant advertising outlays, although such firms may place ads in smaller regional newspapers and church bulletins.

In addition, firms in many of the industries under examination provide their services in the consumer's home. Thus, bonding signals in the form of fancy, imposing office sites would not prove very effective. Many of the remaining service industries perform repair functions, where the physical plant is likely to be a basic facility readily transferrable to other uses. There is, however, one form of advertising in this sector that might perform a signaling function. This is Yellow Pages advertising.

a.. Yellow Pages Advertising

For many consumers, the Yellow Pages will provide the first and sometimes only step in the search process. Firms that wish to stand out in the crowd of listings must pay a substantial

---

[8] The signaling literature is exceedingly complex, and the various signaling models often incorporate critical assumptions specifying precise consumer knowledge of firms' marginal and fixed costs. If these assumptions are relaxed, a positive relationship between quality and advertising or other signals need not be reached in equilibrium. In the words of a recent survey article, "Anything can happen." [5], p. 34.

premium for full and half-page ads. Specifically, a full-page ad in the Suburban Maryland Yellow Pages costs about $42,000 a year.[9] Reaching the entire Washington D.C. area with full-page ads would cost over $100,000 annually.

Although Yellow Pages advertising does incorporate some of the features of a signaling mechanism, it is not a particularly strong test of the theory. Specifically, in a community with high population turnover such as the greater Washington, D.C. region, it is not obvious that the cost of conspicuous Yellow Pages ads would be so high as to require extensive repeat business to justify the investment. The payoff from attracting more first-time, and only-time, purchasers who are new to the region may well be sufficient to warrant such advertising. Indeed, short-term gains may be high enough even in the absence of high population turnover.

In addition, heavy outlays for a large Yellow Pages ad would not be a feasible or even desirable strategy for many firms in the local service sector economy. The service industries at issue are a mixture of small regional providers who serve only a single jurisdiction or even neighborhood, and area-wide firms with perhaps many outlets located in Virginia, Maryland, and the District. Although both types of firms clearly compete with one another, most of the smaller providers may purposefully limit their scale of operation. Such small, localized firms may have no interest in running a very large Yellow Pages ad. Rather, their marketing strategy would be to rely on repeat purchases from current clients and word-of-mouth advertising in their local market area, and to confine their Yellow Pages presence to a single line listing. (In the statistical analysis reported below, the relationship between Yellow Page advertising and quality is explored using both the full sample of firms and a subset of firms that excludes single line listings.)

b. Franchise and National Chain Status

As mentioned previously, a small subset of the studied industries contains firms that are franchisees of a national manufacturer or are members of a national chain. Franchised dealerships are most common in the auto repair sector. There are also several national auto repair chains represented in the Washington, D.C. area (*e.g.* Goodyear, Merchant Tire, Sears, and Jiffy Lube.) National chains or dealerships are present to a lesser extent in the auto body repair, pest control, and major appliance repair industries.

National chains, such as Sears and Jiffy Lube, advertise extensively and enjoy considerable brand name recognition. The non-informational component of these advertising investments can be construed as a pure signal to consumers that the local chain representative

---

[9] This information was provided to the author by Marc Rysman from a data set containing pricing information for almost all Yellow Pages directories in the United States in 1997. See M. Busse and M. Rysman,"Competition and Price Discrimination in Yellow Pages Advertising" Working Paper Series ES, Number 13, Yale School of Management, June 2001.

will satisfy its customers, either in terms of the absolute quality of the service or in terms of quality adjusted for price.

Franchised car dealerships (*e.g.* Toyota, BMW, etc.) may benefit from any goodwill associated with the automobiles they represent, and consumers may assume that dealers have special expertise in repairing their brands of cars. (It should be noted, however, that the potential quality clue offered by franchise status does not constitute a pure signal in the economic sense, since its utility rests on direct information concerning the known quality of the automobile brand and logical inferences concerning the likely expertise a dealership would gain from specializing in the repair of a limited number of automobile brands.)

The hypotheses that chain or dealership affiliation is a reliable indicator of quality or value can be readily tested with the WCC data, since such affiliations are obvious from the title of the firm. Separate zero-one dummy variables were constructed for dealer and chain status, and included as a right-hand term in regressions using WCC quality ratings as a dependent variable.

2. Firm Size

Many consumers may also make quality inferences based on a service provider's size. Size is not a pure signal in the sense described above, since size is a highly complex market outcome rather than a simple short-term investment decision. Further, the relationship between size and quality (as well as price) is an interesting and important economic issue irrespective of whether consumers know a firm's scale of operations or make use of any information they might have. The fundamental question, of course, is whether large size is in fact a market reward for superior performance.

Firms might prosper simply by providing above-average quality at a higher-than-average price, assuming there was a substantial market for such a combination of price and quality. Alternatively, firms may attempt to grow by exploiting any scale economies in such activities as purchasing, inventorying, certain administrative functions, and scheduling. A priori, it is not clear what absolute level of quality would be optimal for such firms. Presumably, however, these providers would attempt to obtain increased market share by passing at least some of their cost savings through to consumers, and we would therefore expect the price charged for any given level of service quality to be below the industry average for that quality level.[10] The WCC data allow us to test whether larger firms offer higher quality, and/or whether such firms offer higher value as measured by consumer quality ratings adjusted for price.

---

[10] This is the outcome that <u>Bond</u> *et al.* [3] observed in their analysis of optometrists operating in states that did and did not allow price advertising and large chain operations. In nonrestrictive states, advertisers provided slightly less thorough eye exams than did smaller nonadvertisers, but charged substantially less for the bundled combination of eye glasses and eye exams.

3. Third Party Certification and Endorsement

Official authorizations, accreditation, or certification from various private or public sources may provide consumers with very straightforward indicators of firm quality. For the local services in this data set, such third party certifications are most prevalent in the auto repair industry. Examples of private endorsements include approval by the American Automobile Association and certification of mechanics by the National Institute of Automotive Service Excellence. Consumers might also infer a quality advantage for repair shops that are approved by local or state governments for safety and/or emissions inspection and testing. The WCC data contain shop-specific information on such certifications and authorizations, and thus provide one means of testing their usefulness to consumers as quality clues.

C. Price and Quality Performance Over Time

As previously discussed, WCC has evaluated most of the 19 industries included in our sample on several occasions since 1976. The time lapse between evaluations ranges from a minimum of three years to over a decade for the infrequently rated industries. These various snapshots in time allow us to evaluate the stability of an individual firm's price and quality ratings and to measure any trends in an industry's overall performance from its initial assessment to the present. Finally, the availability of multiple data sets for most of the sample industries provides a consistency check for the statistical analysis of price-quality correlations and certain other relationships.

III. DETAILED DESCRIPTION OF DATA SET AND VARIABLES

The data set is comprised of 19 local service industries, which represents every industry with WCC price information and consumer quality ratings. As reported in Table I above, in most instances separate data sets were constructed for each evaluation an industry has received since the magazine began publishing in 1976. There are a total of 60 such data sets.

A typical data set for a given industry would include the following variables taken from the WCC ratings: (1) a price index for each firm as constructed by WCC; (2) the number of complaints on file for a given firm at local consumer protection offices, in certain cases adjusted for the size of firm; (3) the quality rating given by the survey respondents; (4) the number of respondents rating a firm; and (5) two zero-one dummy variables to indicate whether WCC had check rated the firm for quality and/or price.

The respondent quality rating variable requires further elaboration. The survey instrument used by WCC asks consumers to rate a firm on the basis of "overall performance," "doing work properly the first time," and a variety of other performance dimensions, such as "letting you know cost early," "starting and completing work promptly," and in some cases, even "neatness." Unless otherwise noted, all of the results reported below are based on the "overall performance" category. Although the "doing work properly" category is in some sense the most focused measure of a firm's pure competence, excelling in the other dimensions of performance included in the "overall performance" category should impose costs on a firm, and these attributes of performance properly should be viewed as components of quality. (In all cases, however, sensitivity tests were conducted to determine whether an alternative measure of quality would alter the results substantially.)

Within each category of firm performance, consumers may rate a firm as "superior," "satisfactory," or "unsatisfactory." For a majority of industries, WCC reports for at least the "overall performance" category both the percentage of respondents rating the firm superior, and the percentage rating the firm either satisfactory or superior. For six of the industries, however, only the broader "satisfactory or superior" percentage is provided. This omission reduces the variance in the quality ratings and could reduce any explanatory power the independent variables might have.

In addition to the WCC variables, supplementary information was gathered for the most recent rating period for 14 of the industries to test for any signaling function provided by Yellow Page advertising. The resulting variable is simply the size of a given firm's advertisement measured in square inches, with a one line regular print listing coded as .25 square inches, and a bold listing coded as .5 square inches. Thus, this variable has a potential range of .25 to 80 for a full ten-by-eight-inch page.

The WCC data set was also supplemented in certain cases with information on firm size as measured by number of employees. WCC was able to supply this information for a total of seven industries. Finally, dummy variables were created where appropriate to represent whether a firm was a dealership or a franchisee of a national chain. Certain other dummy variables were used in the Auto Repair data set, which is discussed separately below.

IV. STATISTICAL METHODOLOGY

For most of the regression analysis reported below, the left-hand variable is the WCC overall performance rating, which is the percentage of survey respondents rating a firm superior (or, in some cases, either satisfactory or superior). There are a number of statistical issues involved in use of this measure as a dependent variable. First, the measure can only vary from zero (percent) at a minimum to 100 at a maximum. Further, a substantial number of summary ratings cluster at or near the upper end of the scale. Under such circumstances, ordinary least squares is not a suitable estimation technique, since the error terms will not be distributed normally.

In addition, the error terms for observations within any given firm will be correlated, since there will be variables not included in our analysis that will have an impact on the overall level of satisfaction ratings for each firm. One such factor could be the politeness and general demeanor of the staff. Firms faring well in this dimension will receive higher WCC quality ratings, which means that a regression that did not capture this determinant of satisfaction would systematically underestimate the quality scores reported by respondents for such firms.

Finally, the number of respondents rating a particular firm varies widely within industries, from a minimum of ten to a maximum of 500 or more. Since these ratings are in effect sample estimates of the true ratings that all customers of that firm would give, the precision of the estimates increases with the number of ratings. It is appropriate, therefore, to weight firm quality ratings by the number of individual ratings on which they are based.

All of these econometric issues were addressed by adopting a logit estimation technique that is structured for use with "grouped" data. In essence, this procedure unfolds the summary quality rating for a given firm into a series of binary categorical variables, with a zero-one value generated for each respondent rating used in calculating the overall quality score. Consider, for example, a firm that receives an overall performance rating of 90, which for most industries would mean that 90 percent of the consumers reporting on that firm rated it superior. If there were a total of 10 respondents, our logit technique would generate a series of dependent variables comprised of nine "one" values and one "zero" value. Each of these dummies would be associated with the corresponding firm-specific independent variables used in the logit regression. Thus, firms with the highest number of individual ratings automatically would be weighted heaviest in the regression estimation procedure. This procedure also adjusts standard errors to correct for the expected correlation of error terms within firms.

V. SUMMARY OF PRINCIPAL FINDINGS

A. Overview of Quality Ratings

Table II below presents the average WCC overall quality ratings for the various industries in the sample for the most recent survey period. The first rating is the average percentage of respondents that gauged the overall performance of firms in the industry as superior. The second rating combines the superior percentage with the percentage of respondents that rated a firm as "adequate." WCC did not disclose ratings for the superior category in six industries, and in four other industries did not provide the combined score for superior and adequate. In the case of restaurants, respondents were asked to rate the quality of the food on a scale of zero to 100. The resulting quality measure therefore is not comparable to the average percentage score ratings for the other industries. Industries are ranked in ascending order by their average rating in the "% Superior or Adequate" category (where available).

Table II
WCC Quality Ratings for Sample Industries

Year Rated	Industry	% Superior	% Superior or Adequate
98	Supermarkets	36.0	------
96	Carpet Installers	-----	80.2
98	Computer Repair	-----	80.2
89	Television Repair	-----	87.7
01	Auto Repair	-----	89.1
96	Appliance Repair	-----	89.8
99	Pest Control	59.6	90.5
98	Auto Body Repair	69.3	90.5
96	Watch Repair	74.5	91.1
98	Plumbers	-----	91.8
97	AC & Heating	70.7	92.9
96	Drycleaners	61.4	94.0
98	Local Movers	69.4	-----
98	Carpet Cleaning	73.7	-----
96	Electricians	78.2	94.4
99	Locksmiths	79.5	95.8
95	Shoe Repair	81.0	-----
99	Tree Experts	79.9	96.5
98	Restaurants	-----	75.4*

*Restaurants are rated on a scale of 0-100

Table II reveals a few interesting patterns and conclusions. First, using the more sensitive "% Superior" rating, Washington area customers are clearly not extremely enthusiastic about the overall quality of local supermarkets. It is not clear whether this reflects an underlying problem, or merely the extreme familiarity consumers have with the food shopping experience. And, for whatever reason, local consumers do seem enthusiastic about their choice of shoe repair firm. Between these two boundaries, industries specializing in mechanical repair do not fare as well as the more traditional "guild" industries, such as electricians, locksmiths, and, as mentioned, shoe repair.

On an overall basis, the various ratings suggest that the local service sector is functioning fairly well from an absolute standpoint. An average of 90 percent of consumers rated their service provider as at least adequate, and an average of 69 percent graded the performance as superior. At a minimum, these percentages do not suggest a major market meltdown of the magnitude associated with a "lemons" model outcome.

B. Consistency of WCC Quality Ratings and Complaint Data

As discussed, the WCC ratings list the number of complaints on file at local consumer protection offices for each rated firm. For certain industries, this number is normalized for firm size, as measured by number of employees. The complaint variable was included in the initial regression runs to function as a possible consistency check on the WCC quality ratings. Since a firm's complaint history is really an indirect measure of quality, it cannot be construed properly as a true independent variable in any regression that uses the WCC quality ratings as a dependent variable. It does have the potential, however, to shed some light on the reliability of the respondent ratings.

In particular, the complaint variable can help determine whether the WCC quality ratings are hopelessly biased by the possibly perverse impact that a firm's prices might have on consumer attitudes toward the firm. As described earlier, this interaction between price and consumer satisfaction, combined with possible selection biases, might yield a strong negative correlation between price and quality, even when true quality was in fact directly related to price.

Consumers presumably take the trouble to write complaint letters over what is perceived as truly egregious firm behavior. Although these complaints may involve what a consumer feels is an exorbitant price, complaints should not be generated by the more subtle impact that, say, a somewhat above-average service repair charge price might have on the disposition of a WCC respondent rating the overall performance of a firm. Thus, the complaint rate variable should help flag firms that are genuinely poor performers, and this variable should be negatively associated with the WCC ratings if these ratings are at all reliable.

The results indicate that there is in fact a persistent and strong negative correlation between firm complaint histories and the quality ratings. For the most recent rating periods, WCC provided some form of complaint data for 14 of the 19 industries. In ten cases, the data were adjusted by firm employee size. In seven of these industries, the complaint rate was negatively and significantly correlated with quality. In the three remaining industries, the coefficient sign was negative but not significant. For five industries, WCC provided only the absolute number of complaints a firm had on file. The complaint coefficients for three of these industries were negative and significant, and insignificant in the remaining two. In the entire data base, the complaint rate variable was negative and significant in approximately 90 percent of the industries for which size-adjusted data were provided. These results, though far from conclusive, do suggest that the WCC ratings are at least flagging the very worst performers.

C. Simple Price-Quality Correlations

In this section, we discuss the threshold question of whether price by itself provides a reliable indicator of quality as measured by WCC respondent performance ratings. The regressions reported do not control for any firm characteristic, such as size or status as a franchisee or dealership, or any signaling mechanism, such as Yellow Pages advertising. The analysis simply attempts to determine the extent to which consumers can rely upon price alone as an indicator of firm quality.

The results of the simple quality-price regressions for the most recent ratings period are reported in Table III. The coefficients were obtained by grouped logit analysis using the WCC quality rating as the dependent variable. P values for the price coefficients appear in parentheses.

TABLE III
Quality-Price Correlations in Most Recent Rating Period

Industry	Coefficient Sign for Price (P-value)
Carpet Cleaning	Positive (.009)
Carpet Installers	Positive (.090)
Dry Cleaning	Positive (.102)
Local Movers	Positive (.216)
Pest Control	Positive (.000)
Restaurants	Positive (.000)
Supermarkets	Positive (.000)
Tree Experts	Positive (.403)
Auto Body Shops	Negative (.548)
Air Conditioning-Htg.	Negative (.034)
Appliance Repair	Negative (.000)
Auto Mechanical Repair	Negative (.000)
Computer Repair	Negative (.078)
Electricians	Negative (.001)
Locksmiths	Negative (.003)
Plumbers	Negative (.007)
Shoe Repair	Negative (.131)
Television Repair	Negative (.307)
Watch Repair	Negative (.732)

As hypothesized, those industries with particularly low search costs and relatively frequent purchase generally display significant positive correlations between price and quality. These are Carpet Cleaning, Restaurants, Supermarkets, and, just missing significance at the .10 level, Dry Cleaning (P=.102). In addition, price and quality are also positively correlated for Carpet Installers and Pest Control. The most striking feature of Table III, however, is the relentless procession of negative correlations in the eleven repair industries, seven of which are significant.

The picture does not change substantially when results for all of the ratings periods are considered. Table IV provides a detailed listing of the observed price-quality correlations for each of the 60 data sets in the sample. Table IV reveals significant positive correlations in ten data sets, representing seven industries. Of these industries, however, only Carpet Cleaning, Drycleaners, and Restaurants are consistently positive over time. Supermarkets reports a highly significant positive price-quality correlation in the two later ratings periods, but is insignificant in 1979. Significant negative price-quality correlations can be observed in 22 data sets, accounting for ten industries, and 28 sets display no significant price-quality correlation.

The widespread occurrence of negative price-quality correlations is difficult to rationalize using any rigorous theory of market performance. Even in the presence of extremely high search costs, there are no *a priori* grounds for expecting price to serve as a *perverse* indicator of quality. Rather, we would simply expect a great deal of noise with no systematic relationship between price and quality. If we are to believe the results reported above, firms apparently prosper by choosing a strategy of high prices and poor performance. It is implausible that even serious market imperfections would perpetually reward such a strategy.[11] Thus, we certainly cannot dismiss the hypothesis that the WCC data are biased due to the previously discussed interaction between price and consumer satisfaction with firm performance.

One alternative hypotheses for certain industries in the sample is that the simple quality and price regressions fail to control for relevant firm cost variables, particularly higher rental

---

[11] Such an outcome might occur under the extreme assumptions that consumers never purchase a service more than once and that absolutely no quality information is available pre-purchase. In that event, some firms might successfully pursue a strategy of high price and low quality, since consumers seeking high quality might specifically target firms quoting the highest price for a service, and by assumption such firms would never be punished for failing to deliver the expected quality. Once these assumptions are relaxed to allow for at least some repeat purchases and limited availability of quality information, it is once again difficult to understand how the high price-low quality strategy could persist so consistently in so many industries over such a long period of time.

Table IV
Quality-Price Correlations for All Industries and Ratings Periods

Industry	Year	Sign	P Value	Observations
AC & Heating Contractors	97	negative	.034	119
	92	negative	.273	106
	87	negative	.428	78
	82	negative	.518	61
	77	positive	.972	44
Appliance Repair	96	negative	.000	46
	91	negative	.002	43
	85	negative	.012	52
	78	negative	.228	60
Auto Body Repair	98	negative	.548	120
	95	negative	.422	106
	90	negative	.393	90
	85	negative	.191	105
	82	negative	.041	71
Auto Mech. Repair	01	negative	.000	482
	97	negative	.000	444
	94	negative	.000	431
	91	negative	.000	380
	88	negative	.000	354
	85	negative	.000	310
	81	negative	.000	289
	76	negative	.004	148
Carpet Cleaning	98	positive	.009	33
	94	positive	.425	31
	87	positive	.727	30
Carpet Sales, Installation	96	positive	.090	24
	89	negative	.723	39
Computer Repair	98	negative	.078	27
	94	positive	.248	31
	89	negative	.929	14

Table IV (Continued)

Industry	Year	Sign	P Value	Observations
Drycleaners	96	positive	.102	211
	90	positive	.038	232
Electricians	96	negative	.001	36
	90	negative	.036	21
Locksmiths	99	negative	.003	25
	94	negative	.499	27
	86	negative	.587	33
Movers	98	positive	.216	28
	92	negative	.720	29
	81	positive	.051	25
Pest Control	97	positive	.000	51
	93	positive	.477	37
	86	negative	.292	46
	77	negative	.030	25
Plumbers	95	negative	.007	134
	89	negative	.045	81
	83	negative	.019	97
	77	positive	.165	58
Restaurants	98	positive	.000	672
	95	positive	.000	718
Shoe Repair	95	negative	.131	95
	88	positive	.213	96
Supermarkets	01	positive	.000	8
	92	positive	.079	7
	79	positive	.997	16
Television Repair	89	negative	.307	36
Tree Experts	99	positive	.403	29
Watch Repair	96	negative	.691	41
	91	negative	.181	30
	80	negative	.002	52

costs in more convenient and/or affluent locations. Consumers presumably would willingly pay more for a tune up in a shop or dealership located close to work or home than one in an industrial park in an outer suburb. Thus, the simple correlations potentially suffer from a missing demand variable in the form of convenience, and a missing supply variable in the form of rental costs. This defect would affect a fairly small number of the sample industries, since so many of the services studied here are performed in the home and do not involve consumer visits to provider sites.

In an attempt to remedy this problem, census household income data by census tract were collected and used as an independent variable in a separate price equation for the relevant industries.[12] Although direct rental cost information by, say, zip code would have been preferable to the income variable, these data were not available. It was hoped that the income data would be sufficiently correlated with rentals to provide a satisfactory substitute. For whatever reason, however, none of the price equations produced significant results, and no subsequent attempt was made to estimate a reduced form equation that would control for convenience and rental costs.

D. Tests of Signaling Theories and the Performance of Larger Firms

Our data set allows tests of several signaling mechanisms, and also a test for whether firm size is associated with quality. The variables and hypothesized outcome for size of Yellow Pages ad, dealership status, and franchisee status have been discussed earlier. In addition, the Auto Repair and Pest Control data sets permit certain other signaling tests that will be discussed separately. Results were obtained from grouped logit regressions that used only the independent variable under examination as a predictor of quality. This specification is appropriate to test the hypothesis that consumers can rely upon the variable of interest in isolation as a signal of quality. See Appendix A for a presentation of the full regression results underlying the discussion in this section.

1. Yellow Pages Advertising

Data on the size of Yellow Pages ads were collected for the most recent rating period for 14 of the 19 industries. This variable was used in several specifications to test for robustness and any extreme value problems that could be introduced by the very wide range in values (from .25 to 80), and the possibility that one or two firms with full page ads might by chance carry particularly high or low quality ratings. Specifically, additional regressions were run with the Yellow Pages variable in log form, and subsets of firms were tested to determine whether any relationship between quality and advertising was limited to advertisements above or below a certain size. In particular, runs were always made excluding firms with one-line listings. As

---

[12] These industries were Auto Body Repair, Auto Mechanical Repair, Drycleaners, Shoe Repair, and Watch Repair. Due to resource constraints and the strong positive price-quality correlation already evident, data were not collected for Restaurants.

discussed earlier, such firms might deliberately have chosen to limit their scale of operation and would never have considered signaling quality using a larger Yellow Pages ad.

The results provide little support for a Yellow Pages signaling function. A significant positive coefficient was found for only four of the 14 industries. In seven industries, the Yellow Pages variable was negatively and significantly associated with quality. There was no significant relationship in the remaining three industries. Simple regressions were also run to investigate whether the size of an ad might signal higher value as measured by the ratio of the quality rating to the price index. None of these regressions supported this hypothesis. Indeed, a significant negative correlation between Yellow Pages ad size and value was found in five industries.

2. Dealership and Franchisee Status

In two industries, Auto Mechanical Repair and Auto Body Repair, numerous firms in the sample were franchised dealerships for the major auto companies. In four industries (the two auto repair industries, Local Movers, and Pest Control), many of the firms were franchisees for national chains, such as Maaco, Sears, United Van Lines, and Orkin Exterminating. In these industries, dummy variables were used to test whether consumers rated such firms higher than independent firms. The results were uniformly negative. The coefficients on these variables were always negative, and usually highly significant. (The results for Auto Mechanical Repair will be presented in more detail below.) Although franchised dealerships consistently charged more than non-dealers, the prices of national chains did not differ significantly from those of independent providers.

3. Firm Size

The firm size variable is of interest for two reasons. First, it clearly would be interesting to see whether larger firms might have attained their size advantage because they provided superior quality. Second, it is of interest to determine whether larger firms are realizing scale economies that might be passed on to consumers in lower prices for a given level of quality. For this data set, the answer to both questions is a resounding no. WCC provided employee size information for seven industries, and in all seven industries there is a very significant negative correlations between quality and size. Nor did larger firms provide greater value in terms of quality adjusted for price. The coefficient on the value variable was negative in all cases, and significantly so in five industries.

4. Warranties

One of the industries–Pest Control–provides a unique opportunity to test whether the length of warranty protection that firms provide signals higher reliability, or whether the warranty functions purely as indemnification in the event of actual product failure. The WCC ratings for pest control firms contain a detailed breakdown of firm charges and terms for a pest eradication treatment for a typical house. WCC lists the initial charge for the treatment, the time period during which the firm will provide a free follow-up treatment, and the charge for treatment after the free follow-up warranty has expired. The warranty varies widely in the sample, from zero days to a full year. Further, as is the case for almost all industries, WCC provides customer ratings for a firm's ability to do the work properly on a first try, as well as an overall performance assessment.

If firms offering longer follow-up warranties were more competent and diligent, so that consumers could rely on the warranty period as an indicator of quality, one would expect that such firms would receive higher ratings for doing the initial treatment properly. This is not the relationship we observe in the Pest Control data set. The rating for doing work properly tends to be negatively and significantly associated with the length of the follow-up treatment warranty.

5. Certification

Finally, the Auto Repair data set contains information that can be used to test whether consumers can rely on various forms of certification and authorization as indicators of quality. WCC indicates for each auto repair establishment whether it is approved by the American Automobile Association, whether the firm employs at least one ASIE technician, and whether it is licensed to perform state safety inspections. The first two variables provide straightforward quality certification tests. The hypothesized coefficient for state safety inspection status is less clear, since many repair establishments may question the profitability of such inspections, and may decline participation for reasons unrelated to provider competence.

Certification by AAA is positively but not significantly correlated with the WCC ratings in the seven auto repair data sets. The ASIE variable, on the other hand, is frequently negative and significant, and never positive and significant. State Safety Inspection facilities consistently fare worse in the quality rankings.

As presented in Appendix A on pp. 43-44, the most dramatic result from the simple regression runs is the strength of the negative correlation between the dealership and chain variables and overall performance. In simple numeric terms, without controlling for any other variables, dealerships on average received an overall satisfaction score of 80.6 in the 1997 ratings, 12 points below the rating of 92.6 for independent shops. Chains, with an average rating of 76.9, scored even lower than dealerships.

Firm size also displays a highly significant negative correlation with quality. Since dealerships and chains tend to be larger than independent shops, it might be concluded that the size variable is merely serving as a proxy for dealership and chain status. As shown in Table V below, however, multivariate regression analysis demonstrates that the significant negative coefficient on firm size persists when dealership and chain status are also included as independent variables.

Further, this negative association between size and quality or between chain status and quality cannot be attributed to any interaction between price and the consumer satisfaction ratings. Price is not correlated with either firm size or chain status in this data set. (Dealerships, however, charged significantly higher prices than independents or chains.) Thus, the negative coefficients for the size and chain variables apparently should be accepted at face value.

TABLE V
Full Regression Results For Auto Repair 1997

Dependent Variable = % rating firm superior or adequate

```
Logit estimates                                 Number of firms =      441.00

                                                LR chi2(7)       =      872.69
                                                Prob > chi2      =      0.0000
Log likelihood = -6423.8417                     Pseudo R2        =      0.0636

----------------------------------------------------------------------------
      supq |     Coef.   Std. Err.       z    P>|z|    [95% Conf. Interval]
-----------+----------------------------------------------------------------
    chain97 |   -1.31156    .097349   -13.47   0.000   -1.502361    -1.12076
   dealer97 |  -.9997785   .0806641   -12.39   0.000   -1.157877   -.8416797
    Price97 |   .0046225   .0015918     2.90   0.004    .0015025    .0077424
      Size7 |  -.0147877   .0034198    -4.32   0.000   -.0214904    -.008085
     ASIE97 |  -.8662402   .2126259    -4.07   0.000   -1.282979   -.4495012
      AAA97 |    .189219   .0550878     3.43   0.001    .0812489     .297189
   Safety97 |  -.3748802   .0612289    -6.12   0.000   -.4948866   -.2548739
   Constant |   3.403598   .2461795    13.83   0.000    2.921095    3.886101
----------------------------------------------------------------------------
```

It should also be noted that the price index variable is positively and significantly correlated with quality in Table V, whereas the coefficient was negative and highly significant when used as a single predictor. The primary explanation for the shift in signs is the explicit accounting for dealer performance in this regression. As discussed, dealers tend to be more expensive and do considerably worse in the ratings than independents. Thus, price acts partially as a proxy for dealership status when used alone as a predictor of quality.

The positive correlation in the full regression cannot, however, be interpreted as an indicator of market efficiency. The reversal in sign merely indicates that we have identified and controlled for one possible source of poor industry performance. On the other hand, the seemingly poor performance of dealers may itself be an artifact of possibly strong selection biases associated with dealership status. For example, if consumers seek out dealers for particularly complicated repair tasks, the probability of service problems inevitably would be higher and reflected in the lower satisfaction ratings.

E. Stability of Price and Quality Ratings Over Time

In this section, we first explore any overall trends in industry quality performance since WCC began its ratings in 1976. (The price data are virtually always normalized, with an average price within any industry assigned a value of 100, and therefore are not suitable for trend analysis.) We then turn to the individual firm level and analyze the stability of firm performance through ratings periods. In particular, we test whether firms that are singled out for a check rating for price or quality tend to maintain a check rating in subsequent periods.

1. Overall Industry Trends

It is of some general interest to determine whether overall performance in the sample service industries has improved over the years, due perhaps to technological improvements or even to the impact of the WCC ratings themselves. There is, unfortunately, a potentially incestuous influence in the WCC data that will tend to improve average satisfaction scores irrespective of any actual increase in quality among all the firms in the industry. Once an industry has been evaluated in an issue of WCC, readers of the magazine can be expected to patronize firms that do well in quality and/or price. In the subsequent rating period, firms that scored poorly initially will tend to receive fewer ratings as readers shift their allegiances to more favored providers, and some will drop out of the sample entirely due to inadequate response rates. Thus, there should be a built-in upward trend in the average quality ratings.

With this proviso, we present in Table VI the results of a simple trend analysis obtained by regressing the average overall satisfaction scores for a given industry on a time counter. In some cases, the number of ratings periods is very low and the resulting "trend" is not particularly interesting. For what they are worth, the results show that, for the 16 industries with more than one WCC rating period, overall satisfaction increases significantly in nine, decreases significantly in four, and displays no trend in three.

TABLE VI
Trends in Service Industry Consumer Satisfaction Over Time

Significant Upward Trend (P<.10): Auto Body Repair, AC & Heating Contractors, Major Appliance Repair, Auto Mechanical Repair, Drycleaning (2 periods), Electricians (2 periods), Locksmiths, Shoe Repair (2 periods), Watch Repair.

Significant Downward Trend: Local Movers, Pest Control, Plumbers, Restaurants.

No Significant Trend: Carpet Cleaning, Carpet Installers, Computer Repair.

---

2. Individual Firm Performance Over Time

Of considerably greater interest than overall industry trends is the issue of whether firms that are singled out for special recognition by WCC for either price or quality tend to repeat their superior performance in the subsequent ratings period. It is possible that some firms might attempt to exploit a quality check rating by, say, lowering costs and quality while maintaining or even increasing price. Similarly, a firm spotlighted for particularly low prices might seek short run gains by increasing prices in the hope that a substantial number of consumers acting on the rating might not realize that the firm had lost its price advantage.

Ideally, we would like to track firm performance shortly after the ratings appeared in order to see the initial impact on what might prove to be short term firm behavior. Because of the long time lag between ratings periods, however, the WCC ratings only allow a check after several years have elapsed. We therefore are limited to assessing any possible direct or indirect long term impact of the ratings on firm performance.

This issue was explored using probit analysis. Specifically, we tested whether firms that were check-rated for price or quality in a given rating period have a greater-than-average probability of being check-rated again in the subsequent period. For any industry with N rating periods, N-1 probits were run so that all subsequent ratings were considered in sequence.

In order to give more intuitive meaning to the probit coefficients, the results are reported in terms of marginal probabilities, which show the *difference* in the probability that a check rated firm vs. a non-check rated firm will receive a check rating in the subsequent period. That is, a marginal probability of .42 indicates that a firm check rated for, say, price in the first period will be 42 percentage points more likely than a non-check rated firm to receive a price check rating in the next period.

The probit analysis provides a more rigorous and meaningful test of any tendency for firms to "milk" reputation effects than would simple comparisons of a firm's price index score or its quality rating between periods. For any given rating period, some firms may tend to score well on the quality survey or price index purely for stochastic reasons. By luck of the draw, an otherwise average firm might find that it had alienated or pleased a particularly large number of consumers who happened to have received the WCC survey form. Similarly, WCC might by happenstance have chosen a mix of service tasks for its price index that particularly advantaged or disadvantaged a firm because of atypical circumstances. A plumbing contractor, for example, might have been short on skilled personnel temporarily on the day WCC requested an estimate for some nontrivial task, and may have quoted a noncompetitive price.

When such firms were rated again in the next period, such stochastic events would tend to even out, and the firms's ratings would tend to "regress to the mean." Thus, to some extent, we would always expect to find on average that firms check rated for, say, quality in 1992 would score somewhat more poorly in 1998. Similarly, an average firm in 1992 might benefit from chance events and earn a check rating in 1998. We could not conclude from this pattern, however, that check rated firms tend to milk their reputations and lower quality.

The probit analysis controls for such random fluctuations and shows more clearly whether there are real differences in the propensity for check rated and non-check rated firms to score well in the subsequent period. Still, the results do not lend themselves to an unambiguous test of the milking hypothesis. In the example above, a significant marginal probability of .42 would indicate that there is no pervasive tendency for firms to shirk once a check rating is achieved. But it would not reject the hypothesis that some firms behave in this manner.

Tables VII presents the probit results for the price and quality ratings. In the column labeled Marginal Probability, the first number represents the marginal probability that firms check rated in the earliest ratings period will repeat their performance in the next rating period. The second number is the marginal probability based on the third vs. second rating period, and so forth. Thus, for an industry that WCC has rated on N occasions, there will be N-1 entries in this column. (The various marginal probabilities were not generated when the initial probit equation showed no significant difference between the probabilities that check rated and uncheck rated firms would be check rated in the next period. Two industries, TV Repair and Tree Experts, do not appear in Table VII because WCC has rated member firms only once. Restaurants and Supermarkets are excluded because WCC did not check rate firms for either price or quality. Thus, the total number of industries in Table VII is 15.)

Table VII shows that firm quality performance is considerably more consistent over timethan price performance. This is not surprising given inevitable measurement errors and other problems in the WCC price index data set. Nevertheless, the price probits reveal a fair amount of consistency in firm ratings. For four industries, the marginal probabilities for all rating periods are significant, and usually highly so. There are mixed results in five industries, with significant marginal probabilities in six periods, six periods with insignificant results, and one period with insufficient observations to permit probit analysis. In one industry, Auto Body Repair, all periods were insignificant. For the remaining four industries, there were either an insufficient number of observations or firms were not check rated for price.

The consistency of firm quality performance is much more impressive. Eleven industries report all marginal probabilities significant in all periods where sample sizes permit probit analysis. One industry, Watch Repair, displayed mixed results. Three industries with small sample sizes report no periods with significant results.

TABLE VII
Probability That Firms Check Rated For Price or Quality Will Be Check Rated in Subsequent Evaluation Period

Industry*	Period	Marginal Probability, Price Check	P Value	Marginal Probability, Quality Check	P Value
Auto Body Repair	82-85	-----	>.10	.645	.000
	85-95	-----	>.10	.353	.005
	95-98	-----	>.10	.536	.000
AC & Heating Contractors	77-82	-----	>.10	Insufficient Observations	
	82-87	-----	>.10	.477	.000
	87-92	.334	.010	.423	.000
	92-97	.450	.000	.350	.020
Appliance Repair	78-85	.485	.025	.484	.000
	85-91	.440	.047	.423	.009
	91-96	.590	.001	.409	.025
Auto Mechanical Repair	76-81	----	NA**	.550	.000
	81-85	.325	.000	.543	.000
	85-88	.330	.000	.492	.000
	88-91	.341	.000	.650	.000
	91-94	.449	.000	.657	.000
	94-97	.367	.000	.555	.000
Carpet Cleaners	87-94	----	>.10	Insufficient Observations	
	94-98	.620	.013	.340	.024
Carpet Installers	89-96	Insufficient Observations		----	>.10
Computer Repair	89-94	Insufficient Observations		Insufficient Observations	
	94-98	.576	.045	.420	.080
Drycleaners	90-96	No Price Check Variable		.430	.000

TABLE VII (Cont.)
Probability That Firms Check Rated For Price or Quality Will Be Check Rated in Subsequent Evaluation Period

Industry	Period	Marginal Probability, Price Check	P Value	Marginal Probability, Quality Check	P Value
Electricians	90-96	Insufficient Observations		.500	.041
Local Movers	81-92	Insufficient Observations		----	>.10
	92-98	Insufficient Observations		Insufficient Observations	
Locksmiths	86-94	----	>.10	Insufficient Observations	
	94-99	.420	.070	----	>.10
Pest Control	77-86	----	>.10	Insufficient Observations	
	86-93	----	.10	Insufficient Observations	
	93-97	.544	.009	.681	.000
Plumbers	77-83	.260	.009	.561	.000
	83-89	.250	.050	.268	.020
	89-95	.174	.100	.467	.000
Shoe Repair	88-95	.451	.001	.283	.041
Watch Repair	89-91	Insufficient Observations		----	>.10
	91-96	No Price Check Variable		.470	.002

*Only one ratings period available for TV Repair and Watch Repair. No Price Check or Quality Check variables available for Supermarkets.

**Firms not check rated separately for price in 1976 ratings.

VII. CONCLUSIONS

The results of this Working Paper paint a very mixed picture of the economic performance of the consumer service sector in the Washington D.C. area. Judging strictly from the absolute levels of satisfaction reported by respondents to the <u>Washington Consumer Checkbook</u> questionnaires, consumers appear reasonably happy with the quality of the services they are receiving. Although the data do not allow any rigorous conclusions in this regard, the observed average satisfaction levels indicate that the service sector has avoided anything resembling a "lemons" equilibrium, where only poor quality is provided.

Market efficiency appears much lower, however, when analyzed more formally using the degree of correlation between price and quality as a benchmark. Only a few industries display positive price-quality correlations that are statistically significant and consistent over time. Of even more concern, the plurality of industries report consistently significant *negative* price-quality correlations. This outcome is contrary to any accepted economic theory of markets, and also fails on common sense grounds. There is no reason to believe that the market would perpetually reward the worst performing firms in an industry.

Thus, it is difficult to reject that conclusion that there are data problems afoot. Specifically, respondents to the WCC survey may to some extent be allowing their satisfaction with the price that is charged for a service color their appraisal of the quality of that service. In effect, consumers may be providing "value" rankings rather than absolute quality rankings. This could explain why the WCC quality ratings frequently appear to fall as price increases.

Any such interaction between price and quality ratings cannot, however, explain other results in our study that are inconsistent with certain theories posited in the literature on the economics of information. Irrespective of price, firms that advertise intensively by running large Yellow Pages displays do not perform better in the WCC ratings, and frequently do more poorly than firms that just run simple one-line listings.

In addition, consumers cannot rely on the relative size of a firm as a clue to probable performance. On average, larger firms score lower than smaller firms on quality, and do not differ significantly on price. Nor does affiliation with a national chain or status as a franchised dealership for a manufacturer signal higher quality. Indeed, in the automobile industry, such firms score much lower in consumer satisfaction than do independent service establishments. Finally, in the one industry were data are available, the length of warranty protection offered for a service does not serve as a signal of higher quality.

Our analysis of time series data for firm price and quality performance shows a fairly high level of consistency in the ratings, particularly for quality. Firms that WCC singles out for quality check rating in one rating period display a much higher probability of receiving a check rating in the next period than do firms that initially are not check rated. Thus, in the long run, it does not appear that most firms "milk" any reputation advantage from the WCC ratings by lowering quality.

Overall conclusions are difficult, particularly because of the potentially serious bias introduced by an interaction between price and the WCC quality rankings. It does appear, however, that consumers in the Washington D.C area have a higher probability of reporting a favorable quality assessment to <u>Washington Consumer Checkbook,</u> if they patronize smaller independent service providers and rely on word-of-mouth reputation rather than Yellow Pages displays, or other indirect clues such as firm size, affiliation with a national chain, or status as a franchised dealership.

REFERENCES

1. AKERLOF, GEORGE A., (1970), "The Market for 'Lemons': Quality Uncertainty and the Market Mechanism," Quarterly Journal of Economics 84, 488-500.

2. ARCHIBALD, ROBERT B., CLYDE A HAULMAN, and CARLISLE E MOODY, JR., (1983), "Quality, Price, Advertising, and Published Quality Ratings," Journal of Consumer Research 9, 347-356.

3. BOND, RONALD S., ET AL., (1980), "Effects of Restrictions On Advertising and Commercial Practices In the Professions: The Case of Optometry," Staff Report to the Federal Trade Commission, Washington, D.C.

4. BUTTERS, GERARD R., (1977), "Equilibrium Distribution of Sales and Advertising Prices," Review of Economic Studies 44, 465-491.

5. CAVES, RICHARD E., and DAVID P. GREENE, (1996), "Brands' Quality Levels, Prices, and Advertising Outlays: Empirical Evidence on Signals and Information Costs," International Journal of Industrial Organization 14, 29-52.

6. GERSTNER, EITAN, (1985), "Do Higher Prices Signal Higher Quality?," Journal of Marketing Research 22, 209-215.

7. GEISTFELD, LOREN V., (1988), "The Price Quality Relationship: The Evidence We Have, The Evidence We Need," The Frontier of Research in The Consumer Interest, ACCI: 143-172.

8. IPPOLITO, PAULINE M., (1990), "Bonding and Nonbonding Signals of Product Quality," Journal of Business 63, 41-60.

9. KLEIN, BENJAMIN, and KEITH B. LEFFLER, (1981), "The Role of Market Forces in Assuring Contractual Performance," Journal of Political Economy 89, 615-641.

10. MORRIS, RUBY TURNER, and CLAIRE SEKULSKI BRONSON, (1969), "The Chaos of Competition Indicated by Consumer Reports," Journal of Marketing 33, 26-34.

11. NELSON, PHILLIP, (1974), "Advertising as Information," Journal of Political Economy 81, 729-754.

12. OXENFELDT, ALFRED R., (1950), "Consumer Knowledge: Its Measurement and Extent," Review of Economics and Statistics, 32, 300-314.

13. ROTHCHILD, MICHAEL, (1973), "Models of Market Organization with Imperfect Information: A Survey," Journal of Political Economy 81, 1283-1308.

14. ROTHCHILD, MICHAEL, and JOSEPH STIGLITZ, (1976), "Equilibrium in Competitive Insurance Markets: An Essay on the Economics of Imperfect Information," Quarterly Journal of Economics 90, 629-650.

15. SPENCE, MICHAEL, (1974), "Competitive and Optimal Responses to Signals: An Analysis of Efficiency and Distribution," Journal of Economic Theory 7, 296-332.

16. STIGLER, GEORGE J., (1961), "The Economics of Information," Journal of Political Economy 69, 213-225.

APPENDIX A
DETAILED REGRESSION RESULTS

This appendix presents the principal regression results for the most recent ratings period for all industries in the data set. As explained in the main text (see pp. 13-14), the regressions that use the WCC quality ratings as a dependent variable employ a form of logit estimation suitable for use with grouped data. In essence, this procedure unfolds the summary quality rating for a given firm into a series of binary categorical variables, with a zero-one value generated for each respondent rating used in calculating the overall quality score.

Consider, for example, a firm that receives an overall performance rating of 80. For most industries this would mean that 80 percent of the consumers reporting on that firm rated it superior in overall performance. If there were a total of 10 respondents, the logit program would generate a series of dependent variables comprised of eight "one" values and two "zero" values. Each of these dummies would be associated with the corresponding firm-specific independent variables used in the logit regression. Thus, firms with the highest number of individual ratings automatically would be weighted heaviest in the regression estimation procedure. The estimation technique also adjusts standard errors to reflect the expected correlation of error terms among the observations for any given service provider.

The discussion first focuses on regressions that include each of the principal independent variables separately as predictors of the WCC quality score. These bivariate regressions test whether consumers can rely on the attribute in question in isolation as a signal of quality. For the Yellow Pages and firm size variables, regression results are also shown testing the hypothesis that consumers can rely upon the size of a Yellow Pages ad or the size of a firm to signal value, as measured by the WCC quality score divided by the WCC price index.

For those industries with a full complement of independent variables, results are then reported for multivariate regressions that reveal more precisely any independent explanatory power that the various variables might have in predicting firm quality. These results are not, however, directly relevant to the primary signaling hypothesis in question, since such theories do not posit that consumers will consciously or unconsciously control for other factors when viewing a single firm attribute as a possible signal of quality.

Air Conditioning and Heating Contractors
(1997)

This data set includes both the Yellow Pages and employment size variables. Regression 1 documents that price and quality are negatively correlated in this industry. In Regression 2, quality and firm size are shown to be negatively correlated at a very high level of significance. Regression 3 shows a positive but insignificant relationship between quality and size of Yellow Pages advertising. Regression 4 indicates that consumers cannot expect a firm with a large

Yellow Pages ad to offer better value in terms of quality per dollar. There is actually a significant negative correlation between these two variables. Regression 5 reveals a negative but insignificant correlation between value (the quality rating adjusted for price) and the size of the firm.

Regression 6 discloses a significant positive relationship between Yellow Pages advertising and quality when firm size and price are also included as independent variables. As is shown in Regression 7, the Yellow Pages variable is positively correlated with price and firm size. Because these two variables are in turn negatively correlated with quality, Yellow Pages functions as a partial proxy for price and size in Regression 3 and loses much of its independent positive correlation with quality.

```
Regression 1:  Dependent Variable = %rating firm superior
               Independent Variable = WCC price index

Logit estimates                              Number of firms =         119
                                             Wald chi2(1)    =        4.49
                                             Prob > chi2     =      0.0340
Log likelihood = -4318.1521                  Pseudo R2       =      0.0047

                           (standard errors adjusted for clustering on idno97)
-------------------------------------------------------------------------------
             |               Robust
       supq  |    Coef.    Std. Err.       z     P>|z|     [95% Conf. Interval]
-------------+-----------------------------------------------------------------
     price97 | -.0098648   .0046538     -2.12    0.034    -.0189861   -.0007435
       _cons |  2.038521   .4890684      4.17    0.000     1.079964    2.997077
-------------------------------------------------------------------------------


Regression 2:  Dependent Variable = %rating firm superior
               Independent Variable = number of employees

Logit estimates                              Number of firms =         134
                                             Wald chi2(1)    =       17.73
                                             Prob > chi2     =      0.0000
Log likelihood = -4936.9785                  Pseudo R2       =      0.0085

                           (standard errors adjusted for clustering on idno97)
-------------------------------------------------------------------------------
             |               Robust
       supq  |    Coef.    Std. Err.       z     P>|z|     [95% Conf. Interval]
-------------+-----------------------------------------------------------------
     employ97| -.0082284   .0019541     -4.21    0.000    -.0120584   -.0043984
       _cons |  1.168227   .0950933     12.29    0.000     .9818473    1.354606
-------------------------------------------------------------------------------
```

Regression 3: Dependent Variable = %rating firm superior
Independent Variable = size of Yellow Pages ad

```
Logit estimates                                Number of firms  =        115
                                               Wald chi2(1)     =       0.17
                                               Prob > chi2      =     0.6767
Log likelihood = -4624.8634                    Pseudo R2        =     0.0002

                        (standard errors adjusted for clustering on idno97)
-------------------------------------------------------------------------------
           |                Robust
     supq  |    Coef.    Std. Err.       z    P>|z|     [95% Conf. Interval]
-----------+-------------------------------------------------------------------
     yp97  |  .0013026    .003124      0.42   0.677    -.0048203     .0074255
    _cons  |  .9231844   .1079349      8.55   0.000      .711636     1.134733
-------------------------------------------------------------------------------
```

Regression 4: Dependent Variable = size of Yellow Pages ad
Independent Variable = value (quality/price)

```
    Source |       SS       df       MS              Number of firms =     102
-----------+------------------------------           F( 1,    100)  =    13.86
     Model | 5610.21758      1   5610.21758          Prob > F        =   0.0003
  Residual | 40478.981     100    404.78981          R-squared       =   0.1217
-----------+------------------------------           Adj R-squared   =   0.1129
     Total | 46089.1985    101   456.328698          Root MSE        =   20.119


-------------------------------------------------------------------------------
     yp97  |    Coef.    Std. Err.       t    P>|t|     [95% Conf. Interval]
-----------+-------------------------------------------------------------------
     value | -45.44601   12.20733     -3.723  0.000    -69.66501    -21.22702
    _cons  |  57.25293   11.50368      4.977  0.000     34.42995     80.07591
-------------------------------------------------------------------------------
```

Regression 5: Dependent Variable = number of employees
Independent Variable = value (quality/price)

```
    Source |       SS       df       MS              Number of firms =     117
-----------+------------------------------           F( 1,    115)  =     1.66
     Model | 401.425903     1   401.425903           Prob > F        =   0.2001
  Residual | 27798.822    115   241.728887           R-squared       =   0.0142
-----------+------------------------------           Adj R-squared   =   0.0057
     Total | 28200.2479   116   243.105585           Root MSE        =   15.548


-------------------------------------------------------------------------------
  employ97 |    Coef.    Std. Err.       t    P>|t|     [95% Conf. Interval]
-----------+-------------------------------------------------------------------
     value | -10.79503   8.376937     -1.289  0.200    -27.38812     5.798074
    _cons  |  26.18363   8.028892      3.261  0.001     10.27994     42.08732
-------------------------------------------------------------------------------
```

Regression 6: Dependent Variable = %rating firm superior
             Independent Variables = number of employees, size of Yellow
                              Pages ad, WCC price index

```
Logit estimates                                    Number of firms =        101
                                                   Wald chi2(3)    =      14.36
                                                   Prob > chi2     =     0.0025
Log likelihood =  -3994.811                        Pseudo R2       =     0.0143

                              (standard errors adjusted for clustering on idno97)
------------------------------------------------------------------------------
             |               Robust
        supq |     Coef.   Std. Err.        z     P>|z|     [95% Conf. Interval]
-------------+----------------------------------------------------------------
    employ97 | -.0141104   .0048582     -2.90    0.004    -.0236323   -.0045885
        yp97 |  .0089862   .0033431      2.69    0.007     .0024337    .0155386
     price97 | -.0148654    .004524     -3.29    0.001    -.0237323   -.0059986
       _cons |  2.647565   .4989876      5.31    0.000     1.669567    3.625562
------------------------------------------------------------------------------
```

Regression 7: Dependent Variable = size of Yellow Pages ad
             Independent Variables = number of employees, WCC price index,
                              %rating firm superior

```
     Source |       SS       df       MS                Number of firms =    101
-------------+------------------------------            F( 3,     97) =    12.87
      Model | 13071.5361        3   4357.1787           Prob > F      =   0.0000
   Residual | 32845.053        97  338.608794           R-squared     =   0.2847
-------------+------------------------------            Adj R-squared =   0.2626
      Total | 45916.5891      100  459.165891           Root MSE      =   18.401


------------------------------------------------------------------------------
        yp97 |     Coef.   Std. Err.        t     P>|t|     [95% Conf. Interval]
-------------+----------------------------------------------------------------
    employ97 |  .4527038   .1165674      3.884    0.000     .2213497    .6840579
     price97 |  .5658379   .1158479      4.884    0.000     .3359119    .7957638
     super97 |  .1546826   .1265388      1.222    0.225    -.0964618     .405827
       _cons | -61.42468   17.26251     -3.558    0.001    -95.68598   -27.16337
------------------------------------------------------------------------------
```

Auto Body Repair
(1998)

The simple two-way regressions for the 1998 Auto Body Repair data set reveal no significant association between price and quality (Regression 1), and highly significant negative correlations between quality and firm size (Regression 2), dealer status (Regression 6), and chain status (Regression 7). (There is only one national chain represented in this data set). Regression 3 reveals no significant relationship between quality and the size of Yellow Pages advertising, and Regression 4 shows that the Yellow Pages variable is not significantly correlated with the value variable (WCC quality score/WCC price index). In Regression 5, there is a highly significant negative correlation between value and size of firm.

With all of the independent variables included in Regression 8, dealer status and chain status continue to display highly significant negative coefficients. Firm size and Yellow Pages advertising lose significance, however, and price remains insignificant. Further investigation revealed that the dealer dummy variable and firm size are positively correlated (r=.42). Thus, when firm size is used as the only regressor, it functions partially as a proxy for dealer status in predicting firm quality. Taken together, the results for the full regression and simple regressions indicate that dealer status is a more powerful predictor of firm quality than is firm size.

In Regression 9, Yellow Pages advertising is removed in order to increase the sample size. (A number of smaller firms rated by WCC could not be located in the Yellow Pages listings.) In the expanded set, firm size achieves a high level of significance, although the z score for dealer status is once again higher than for firm size, and the positive coefficient on the price variable attains significance.

Regression 1: Dependent Variable = %rating firm superior
Independent Variable = WCC price index

```
Logit estimates                           Number of firms =         120
                                          Wald chi2(1)    =        0.36
                                          Prob > chi2     =      0.5480
Log likelihood = -1935.1868               Pseudo R2       =      0.0004

                      (standard errors adjusted for clustering on idno98)
------------------------------------------------------------------------------
             |               Robust
        supq |      Coef.   Std. Err.       z    P>|z|     [95% Conf. Interval]
-------------+----------------------------------------------------------------
       price |  -.0065402    .0108856    -0.60   0.548    -.0278756    .0147953
       _cons |   1.584347    1.106101     1.43   0.152    -.5835702    3.752264
------------------------------------------------------------------------------
```

Regression 2: Dependent Variable = %rating firm superior
Independent Variable = number of employees

```
Logit estimates                           Number of firms =         138
                                          Wald chi2(1)    =       15.09
                                          Prob > chi2     =      0.0001
Log likelihood = -2218.0717               Pseudo R2       =      0.0155

                      (standard errors adjusted for clustering on idno98)
------------------------------------------------------------------------------
             |               Robust
        supq |      Coef.   Std. Err.       z    P>|z|     [95% Conf. Interval]
-------------+----------------------------------------------------------------
     employ98 | -.0558852    .0143885    -3.88   0.000    -.0840862    -.0276842
       _cons |   1.439325    .1341409    10.73   0.000     1.176414    1.702237
------------------------------------------------------------------------------
```

Regression 3: Dependent Variable = %rating firm superior
**   Independent Variable = size of Yellow Pages ad**

Logit estimates   Number of firms =   95
                                                   Wald chi2(1)   =   0.79
                                                   Prob > chi2   =   0.3730
Log likelihood = -1882.6538   Pseudo R2   =   0.0009

                              (standard errors adjusted for clustering on idno98)

             | Robust
        supq | Coef.   Std. Err.   z   P>|z| [95% Conf. Interval]
-------------+--
          yp | -.0083301   .0093499   -0.89   0.373   -.0266556   .0099954
       _cons | 1.04312   .1049185   9.94   0.000   .8374834   1.248756

Regression 4: Dependent Variable = size of Yellow Pages ad
**   Independent Variable = value (quality/price)**

      Source | SS   df   MS   Number of firms =   95
-------------+------------------------------   F(1,   93) =   1.29
       Model | 130.662894   1   130.662894   Prob > F   = 0.2586
    Residual | 9404.25158   93   101.120985   R-squared   = 0.0137
-------------+------------------------------   Adj R-squared = 0.0031
       Total | 9534.91447   94   101.43526   Root MSE   = 10.056

----
          yp | Coef.   Std. Err.   t   P>|t| [95% Conf. Interval]
-------------+--
       value | -6.909842   6.078726   -1.137   0.259   -18.98099   5.161304
       _cons | 12.17246   4.41782   2.755   0.007   3.399545   20.94537

Regression 5: Dependent Variable = number of employees
**   Independent Variable = value (quality/price)**

      Source | SS   df   MS   Number of firms =   120
-------------+------------------------------   F(1,   118) =   25.21
       Model | 558.897059   1   558.897059   Prob > F   = 0.0000
    Residual | 2615.85086   118   22.1682276   R-squared   = 0.1760
-------------+------------------------------   Adj R-squared = 0.1691
       Total | 3174.74792   119   26.6785539   Root MSE   = 4.7083

----
    employ98 | Coef.   Std. Err.   t   P>|t| [95% Conf. Interval]
-------------+--
       value | -12.46466   2.482447   -5.021   0.000   -17.38058   -7.548738
       _cons | 16.65288   1.776893   9.372   0.000   13.13414   20.17161

Regression 6: Dependent Variable = %rating firm superior
        Independent Variable = dealer status (dealer = 1)

```
Logit estimates                                 Number of firms =        138
                                                Wald chi2(1)    =      52.86
                                                Prob > chi2     =     0.0000
Log likelihood = -2187.0624                     Pseudo R2       =     0.0293

                        (standard errors adjusted for clustering on idno98)
------------------------------------------------------------------------------
             |               Robust
        supq |    Coef.    Std. Err.      z     P>|z|    [95% Conf. Interval]
-------------+----------------------------------------------------------------
      dealer | -.9553177    .131402    -7.27   0.000   -1.212861   -.6977746
       _cons |  1.164308   .0762207    15.28   0.000    1.014918    1.313697
------------------------------------------------------------------------------
```

Regression 7: Dependent Variable = %rating firm superior
        Independent Variable = chain status (chain = 1)

```
Logit estimates                                 Number of firms =        138
                                                Wald chi2(1)    =      53.28
                                                Prob > chi2     =     0.0000
Log likelihood = -2242.4496                     Pseudo R2       =     0.0047

                        (standard errors adjusted for clustering on idno98)
------------------------------------------------------------------------------
             |               Robust
        supq |    Coef.    Std. Err.      z     P>|z|    [95% Conf. Interval]
-------------+----------------------------------------------------------------
       chain| -1.216412   .1666463    -7.30   0.000   -1.543033   -.8897911
       _cons |  .9481478   .0802853    11.81   0.000    .7907916    1.105504
------------------------------------------------------------------------------
```

Regression 8 Dependent Variable = %rating firm superior
        Independent Variables = dealer status, wcc price index, size of
                         Yellow Pages ad, number of employees,
                         chain status

```
Logit estimates                                 Number of firms =         95
                                                LR chi2(5)      =     131.31
                                                Prob > chi2     =     0.0000
Log likelihood =  -1546.322                     Pseudo R2       =     0.0407

------------------------------------------------------------------------------
        supq |    Coef.    Std. Err.      z     P>|z|    [95% Conf. Interval]
-------------+----------------------------------------------------------------
      dealer | -1.085687   .1257825    -8.63   0.000   -1.332216   -.8391573
       price |  .0057761   .0067361     0.86   0.391   -.0074264    .0189786
          yp |  .0026465    .006309     0.42   0.675   -.0097188    .0150119
     employ98| -.0178601   .0101569    -1.76   0.079   -.0377674    .0020471
       chain | -1.538303   .3354031    -4.59   0.000   -2.195681   -.8809248
       _cons |  .7754602   .6555708     1.18   0.237   -.5094349    2.060355
------------------------------------------------------------------------------
```

```
Regression 9: Dependent Variable = %rating firm superior
              Independent Variables = dealer status, WCC price index,
                                      number of employees, chain status


Logit estimates                               Number of firms =        120
                                              LR chi2(4)       =     176.25
                                              Prob > chi2      =     0.0000
Log likelihood = -1847.7438                   Pseudo R2        =     0.0455


-------------------------------------------------------------------------------
       supq |    Coef.    Std. Err.      z     P>|z|     [95% Conf. Interval]
------------+------------------------------------------------------------------
     dealer |  -.956223    .1047231    -9.13    0.000    -1.161477    -.7509695
      price |   .010555    .0059654     1.77    0.077    -.0011369     .0222469
   employ98 |  -.0289016   .0080113    -3.61    0.000    -.0446034    -.0131997
      chain |  -1.4128     .2672092    -5.29    0.000    -1.93652     -.8890793
      _cons |   .4006843   .5855493     0.68    0.494    -.7469713    1.54834
-------------------------------------------------------------------------------
```

Auto Mechanical Repair
(1997)

The Automobile Mechanical Repair data set is the largest in the sample, both in terms of the number of firms and the number of possible predictors of firm quality. The results for the full set of independent variables for 1997 have already been discussed in the main text on page 24. The results shown below are for the simple two-way regressions and a regression using size of Yellow Pages advertising as the dependent variable.

Regression 1 reports that price functions as a perverse indicator of quality in this industry. The price coefficient is negative and highly significant. Regression 2 reveals that firm size (as measured by number of employees) is also inversely related to quality. Indeed, all of the remaining signaling variables--size of Yellow Pages ad, dealer status, and chain status–display negative coefficients (Regressions 3, 6, and 7). Regressions (not shown) using dummy variables for various certifications revealed significant negative coefficients for employment of ASIE-certified technicians, and designation as a state safety inspection site, and a positive but insignificant coefficient for certification by the American Automobile Association. Regression 4 reveals a significant negative correlation between size of Yellow Pages ad and value, which is measured by the ratio of the WCC quality score to the WCC price index. In Regression 5, there is a much stronger negative correlation between the value variable and size of firm.

Regression 1: Dependent Variable = %rating firm superior or adequate
**   Independent Variable = WCC price index**

Logit estimates

```
                                         Number of firms  =        444
                                         Wald chi2(1)     =      30.05
                                         Prob > chi2      =     0.0000
Log likelihood = -6770.2166              Pseudo R2        =     0.0131
```

(standard errors adjusted for clustering on comno)

supq	Coef.	Robust Std. Err.	z	P>|z|	[95% Conf. Interval]	
pricin97	-.0159178	.0029039	-5.48	0.000	-.0216093	-.0102262
_cons	3.679106	.3079504	11.95	0.000	3.075534	4.282678

Regression 2: Dependent Variable = %rating firm superior or adequate
**   Independent Variable = number of employees**

Logit estimates

```
                                         Number of firms  =        515
                                         Wald chi2(1)     =      55.66
                                         Prob > chi2      =     0.0000
Log likelihood = -7610.5535              Pseudo R2        =     0.0311
```

(standard errors adjusted for clustering on comno)

supq	Coef.	Robust Std. Err.	z	P>|z|	[95% Conf. Interval]	
employ97	-.0429339	.0057547	-7.46	0.000	-.0542129	-.0316549
_cons	2.583182	.0872403	29.61	0.000	2.412194	2.75417

Regression 3: Dependent Variable = %rating firm superior or adequate
**   Independent Variable = size of Yellow Pages advertisement**

Logit estimates

```
                                         Number of firms  =        321
                                         Wald chi2(1)     =       1.11
                                         Prob > chi2      =     0.2913
Log likelihood =  -4669.489              Pseudo R2        =     0.0004
```

(standard errors adjusted for clustering on comno)

supq	Coef.	Robust Std. Err.	z	P>|z|	[95% Conf. Interval]	
yp97	-.0030682	.0029076	-1.06	0.291	-.0087671	.0026306
_cons	2.154566	.0848792	25.38	0.000	1.988206	2.320926

Regression 4: Dependent Variable = size of Yellow Pages ad
Independent Variable = value (quality/price)

Source	SS	df	MS			
Model	1338.41317	1	1338.41317			
Residual	114319.277	276	414.200277			
Total	115657.69	277	417.536786			

Number of firms =   278
$F(1, 276) = 3.23$
Prob > F   = 0.0733
R-squared   = 0.0116
Adj R-squared = 0.0080
Root MSE   = 20.352

yp97	Coef.	Std. Err.	t	P>|t|	[95% Conf. Interval]	
value	-10.3485	5.756882	-1.798	0.073	-21.68147	.9844806
_cons	19.89839	5.525921	3.601	0.000	9.02008	30.77669

Regression 5: Dependent Variable = number of employees
Independent Variable = value (quality/price)

Source	SS	df	MS			
Model	6026.86996	1	6026.86996			
Residual	18524.6993	442	41.9110844			
Total	24551.5693	443	55.4211496			

Number of firms =   444
$F(1, 442) = 143.80$
Prob > F   = 0.0000
R-squared   = 0.2455
Adj R-squared = 0.2438
Root MSE   = 6.4739

employ97	Coef.	Std. Err.	t	P>|t|	[95% Conf. Interval]	
value	-16.59809	1.384129	-11.992	0.000	-19.31838	-13.8778
_cons	24.0596	1.299164	18.519	0.000	21.50629	26.6129

Regression 6: Dependent Variable = %rating firm superior or adequate
Independent Variable = dealer status

Logit estimates

Log likelihood = -7531.3521

Number of firms =   515
Wald chi2(1)   = 137.69
Prob > chi2   = 0.0000
Pseudo R2   = 0.0412

(standard errors adjusted for clustering on comno)

supq	Coef.	Robust Std. Err.	z	P>|z|	[95% Conf. Interval]	
dealer97	-1.098344	.0936021	-11.73	0.000	-1.281801	-.9148873
_cons	2.591357	.0745284	34.77	0.000	2.445284	2.73743

```
Regression 7:  Dependent Variable = %rating firm superior or adequate
               Independent Variable = chain status

Logit estimates                               Number of firms  =          515
                                              Wald chi2(1)     =        14.35
                                              Prob > chi2      =       0.0002
Log likelihood = -7831.9797                   Pseudo R2        =       0.0029

                           (standard errors adjusted for clustering on comno)
-----------------------------------------------------------------------------
             |               Robust
       supq  |    Coef.    Std. Err.      z     P>|z|    [95% Conf. Interval]
-------------+---------------------------------------------------------------
     chain97 |  -.6145223   .1622175    -3.79   0.000    -.9324628   -.2965818
       _cons |   2.021323   .0574306    35.20   0.000     1.908761    2.133885
-----------------------------------------------------------------------------
```

Carpet Cleaning
(1998)

The only variables in this data set are price and size of Yellow Pages advertisement. Price proves to be positively correlated with quality (Regression 1). Yellow Pages advertising displays an insignificant negative correlation with quality in Regression 2, and with value (quality adjusted for price) in Regression 3.

```
Regression 1:  Dependent Variable = %rating firm superior or adequate
               Independent Variable = WCC price index

Logit estimates                               Number of firms =           33
                                              Wald chi2(1)    =         6.79
                                              Prob > chi2     =       0.0092
Log likelihood = -893.30575                   Pseudo R2       =       0.0470

                          (standard errors adjusted for clustering on comidno)
-----------------------------------------------------------------------------
             |               Robust
       supq  |    Coef.    Std. Err.      z     P>|z|    [95% Conf. Interval]
-------------+---------------------------------------------------------------
     price98 |   .030564    .0117299     2.61   0.009     .0075738    .0535543
       _cons |  -1.467002   1.046967    -1.40   0.161    -3.519019    .5850145
-----------------------------------------------------------------------------
```

```
Regression 2:   Dependent Variable = %rating firm superior or adequate
                Independent Variable = size of Yellow Pages advertisement

Logit estimates                                   Number of firms =        38
                                                  Wald chi2(1)    =      0.91
                                                  Prob > chi2     =    0.3395
Log likelihood = -1129.8918                       Pseudo R2       =    0.0024

                         (standard errors adjusted for clustering on comidno)
-------------------------------------------------------------------------------
             |               Robust
        supq |    Coef.    Std. Err.      z     P>|z|     [95% Conf. Interval]
-------------+-----------------------------------------------------------------
        yp98 | -.0046769   .0048966    -0.96    0.340    -.0142742    .0049203
       _cons |  .7946941   .3790674     2.10    0.036     .0517356   1.537653
-------------------------------------------------------------------------------


Regression 3:   Dependent Variable = size of Yellow Pages Ad
                Independent Variable = value (quality/price)

    Source |       SS       df       MS              Number of firms =      27
-----------+------------------------------           F( 1,    25) =      2.55
     Model |  1285.4712      1   1285.4712           Prob > F      =   0.1230
  Residual |  12611.6723     25  504.466893          R-squared     =   0.0925
-----------+------------------------------           Adj R-squared =   0.0562
     Total |  13897.1435     26   534.50552          Root MSE      =    22.46


-------------------------------------------------------------------------------
        yp98 |    Coef.    Std. Err.      t     P>|t|     [95% Conf. Interval]
-------------+-----------------------------------------------------------------
       value | -19.90948   12.47226    -1.596   0.123    -45.59657    5.777614
       _cons |  34.77875   13.80935     2.518   0.019      6.337861   63.21964
-------------------------------------------------------------------------------
```

Carpet Sales and Installation
(1996)

WCC respondents were asked to rate carpet firms both for the quality of the sales advice given in the showroom and for the quality of any installation services that were provided. This data set does not have any information on firm size. Regressions 1 and 2, respectively, show a significant positive correlation between price and the quality of sales service, and a positive but insignificant correlation between the size of a firm's Yellow Pages ad and respondent satisfaction with the sales services.

With respect to the quality of installation services, Regression 3 reveals no significant relationship between price and quality. Note, however, that the sample size for installation services is considerably smaller than for sales services (24 vs. 36). Regression 4 shows a positive but insignificant association between the size of Yellow Pages ads and satisfaction with installation (P=.124). Further regression analysis (not shown) detected no significant relationship between

Yellow Pages ad size and price, or for quality adjusted for price, using either the sales service or installation service satisfaction measure.

Regression 1:   Dependent Variable = %rating firm adequate or superior
for sales services
Independent Variable = WCC price index

```
Logit estimates                                    Number of firms =          36
                                                   Wald chi2(1)    =        2.88
                                                   Prob > chi2     =      0.0896
Log likelihood = -279.14817                        Pseudo R2       =      0.0191

                             (standard errors adjusted for clustering on idno96)
------------------------------------------------------------------------------
             |               Robust
       supq  |    Coef.    Std. Err.      z     P>|z|     [95% Conf. Interval]
-------------+----------------------------------------------------------------
     price96 |  .0316688   .0186556     1.70    0.090    -.0048956    .0682331
       _cons | -1.001684   1.894259    -0.53    0.597    -4.714365    2.710996
------------------------------------------------------------------------------
```

Regression 2:   Dependent Variable = % adequate or superior, sales services
Independent Variable = size of Yellow Pages ad

```
Logit estimates                                    Number of firms =          42
                                                   Wald chi2(1)    =        0.46
                                                   Prob > chi2     =      0.4966
Log likelihood = -314.43372                        Pseudo R2       =      0.0021

                             (standard errors adjusted for clustering on idno96)
------------------------------------------------------------------------------
             |               Robust
       supq  |    Coef.    Std. Err.      z     P>|z|     [95% Conf. Interval]
-------------+----------------------------------------------------------------
       yp96  |  .0120109   .0176681     0.68    0.497    -.0226181    .0466398
       _cons |  2.197738   .2713814     8.10    0.000     1.665841    2.729636
------------------------------------------------------------------------------
```

Regression 3: Dependent Variable = %adequate or superior, installation
Independent Variable = WCC price index

```
Logit estimates                                    Number of firms =          24
                                                   Wald chi2(1)    =        0.04
                                                   Prob > chi2     =      0.8391
Log likelihood = -249.35669                        Pseudo R2       =      0.0001

                             (standard errors adjusted for clustering on idno96)
------------------------------------------------------------------------------
             |               Robust
       supq  |    Coef.    Std. Err.      z     P>|z|     [95% Conf. Interval]
-------------+----------------------------------------------------------------
     price96 |  .0023001   .0113312     0.20    0.839    -.0199086    .0245088
       _cons |  1.345761   1.146281     1.17    0.240    -.9009087    3.592431
------------------------------------------------------------------------------
```

Regression 4: Dependent Variable = %adequate or superior, installation
Independent Variable = size of Yellow Pages ad

```
Logit estimates                                    Number of firms =        28
                                                   Wald chi2(1)    =      2.33
                                                   Prob > chi2     =    0.1268
Log likelihood = -278.00221                        Pseudo R2       =    0.0063
```

(standard errors adjusted for clustering on idno96)

supq	Coef.	Robust Std. Err.	z	P>|z|	[95% Conf. Interval]	
yp96	.0190109	.0124501	1.53	0.127	-.0053908	.0434127
_cons	1.369419	.1885602	7.26	0.000	.9998473	1.73899

Computer Repair
(1998)

This data set contains only two independent variables--price and Yellow Pages ad size. In Regression 1, price is negatively associated with quality. In Regression 2, no significant correlation is found between quality and the size of a firm's Yellow Pages ad. Further analysis (not shown) revealed a direct and significant correlation between the Yellow Pages variable and price, and no correlation between Yellow Pages ad size and value as measured by quality adjusted for price.

Regression 1: Dependent Variable = %rating firm adequate or superior
Independent Variable = WCC price index

```
Logit estimates                                    Number of firms =        27
                                                   Wald chi2(1)    =      3.10
                                                   Prob > chi2     =    0.0781
Log likelihood = -420.23779                        Pseudo R2       =    0.0152
```

(standard errors adjusted for clustering on comidno)

supq	Coef.	Robust Std. Err.	z	P>|z|	[95% Conf. Interval]	
price98	-.0208608	.0118402	-1.76	0.078	-.0440672	.0023455
_cons	3.439096	1.14026	3.02	0.003	1.204227	5.673964

```
Regression 2:  Dependent Variable = %rating firm adequate or superior
               Independent Variable = size of Yellow Pages ad

Logit estimates                              Number of firms =         18
                                             Wald chi2(1)    =       0.79
                                             Prob > chi2     =     0.3749
Log likelihood = -396.03579                  Pseudo R2       =     0.0109

                        (standard errors adjusted for clustering on comidno)
---------------------------------------------------------------------------
             |                 Robust
        supq |     Coef.    Std. Err.      z    P>|z|     [95% Conf. Interval]
-------------+-------------------------------------------------------------
        yp98 |    .02605    .0293559     0.89   0.375    -.0314865    .0835865
       _cons |  .9515454    .2741594     3.47   0.001     .4142029    1.488888
---------------------------------------------------------------------------
```

Drycleaners
(1996)

The drycleaners data set is one of the largest in the sample, although it does not contain information on firm size. In Regression 1, the price coefficient is positive but just misses significance (P=.102). No significant correlation is found between the size of a firm's Yellow Pages ad and quality in Regression 2. Regression 3 shows that price and Yellow Pages ad size are positively correlated at a high level of significance. There is no relationship between the Yellow Pages variable and value as measured by the WCC quality score divided by the WCC price score (results not shown).

```
Regression 1:  Dependent Variable = %rating firm superior
               Independent Variable = WCC price index

Logit estimates                              Number of firms =        211
                                             Wald chi2(1)    =       2.68
                                             Prob > chi2     =     0.1018
Log likelihood = -2696.4198                  Pseudo R2       =     0.0015

                        (standard errors adjusted for clustering on comidno)
---------------------------------------------------------------------------
             |                 Robust
        supq |     Coef.    Std. Err.      z    P>|z|     [95% Conf. Interval]
-------------+-------------------------------------------------------------
      price96 |  .0043811    .0026777     1.64   0.102    -.0008671    .0096293
       _cons |  .0386459    .2725427     0.14   0.887     -.495528    .5728199
---------------------------------------------------------------------------
```

Regression 2:   Dependent Variable = %rating firm superior
**   Independent Variable = size of Yellow Pages ad**

```
Logit estimates                                Number of firms =        188
                                               Wald chi2(1)    =       2.14
                                               Prob > chi2     =     0.1434
Log likelihood = -2423.9233                    Pseudo R2       =     0.0013

                             (standard errors adjusted for clustering on comidno)
-------------------------------------------------------------------------------
             |                 Robust
      supq   |    Coef.    Std. Err.      z     P>|z|     [95% Conf. Interval]
-------------+-----------------------------------------------------------------
      yp96   |  .0521381   .0356334     1.46    0.143    -.017702     .1219782
     _cons   |  .4273209   .0758077     5.64    0.000     .2787405    .5759013
-------------------------------------------------------------------------------
```

Regression 3:   Dependent Variable = size of Yellow Pages ad
**   Independent Variable = WCC price index**

```
   Source  |      SS         df       MS            Number of firms =      188
-----------+-----------------------------            F( 1,    186)  =    16.60
    Model  |  50.4561121      1   50.4561121         Prob > F        =   0.0001
 Residual  |  565.497013    186   3.04030652         R-squared       =   0.0819
-----------+-----------------------------            Adj R-squared   =   0.0770
    Total  |  615.953125    187   3.29386698         Root MSE        =   1.7436

-------------------------------------------------------------------------------
     yp96  |     Coef.    Std. Err.       t     P>|t|     [95% Conf. Interval]
-----------+-------------------------------------------------------------------
  price96  |   .023579    .005788       4.074   0.000     .0121605    .0349975
    _cons  |  -1.571738   .59892       -2.624   0.009    -2.753288   -.3901887
-------------------------------------------------------------------------------
```

Electricians
(1996)

The data set for electricians is fairly small, but does contain information on firm size as measured by number of employees. Regression 1 reveals a strong negative correlation between price and quality. Further investigation (not shown) detected no correlations between price and any of the other independent variables. Thus, price is not acting as a proxy for, say, firm size. In Regression 2, firm size and quality are not significantly correlated, although there is a significant negative association between quality and size of Yellow Pages ad in Regression 3. Regression 4 shows that the size of a Yellow Pages ad cannot be used as a signal of value. The Yellow Pages variable is negatively correlated with value (as measured by the WCC quality score divided by the WCC price index). In Regression 5, the value variable is also negatively correlated with firm size, but the relationship is not significant.

Regression 1:   Dependent Variable = %rating firm superior
**   Independent Variable = WCC price index**

```
Logit estimates                                 Number of firms =        36
                                                Wald chi2(1)    =     10.87
                                                Prob > chi2     =    0.0010
Log likelihood =  -414.3513                     Pseudo R2       =    0.0314

                           (standard errors adjusted for clustering on comidno)
------------------------------------------------------------------------------
             |               Robust
        supq |     Coef.   Std. Err.      z    P>|z|     [95% Conf. Interval]
-------------+----------------------------------------------------------------
     price96 | -.0164893   .0050023    -3.30   0.001    -.0262937    -.006685
       _cons |  2.993674   .5343611     5.60   0.000     1.946345    4.041002
------------------------------------------------------------------------------
```

Regression 2:   Dependent Variable = %rating firm superior
**   Independent Variable = number of employees**

```
Logit estimates                                 Number of firms =        35
                                                Wald chi2(1)    =      1.65
                                                Prob > chi2     =    0.1996
Log likelihood = -383.62685                     Pseudo R2       =    0.0061

                           (standard errors adjusted for clustering on comidno)
------------------------------------------------------------------------------
             |               Robust
        supq |     Coef.   Std. Err.      z    P>|z|     [95% Conf. Interval]
-------------+----------------------------------------------------------------
    employ96 | -.0323265   .0252028    -1.28   0.200    -.0817232    .0170701
       _cons |  1.596658   .1849404     8.63   0.000     1.234182    1.959135
------------------------------------------------------------------------------
```

Regression 3:   Dependent Variable = %rating firm superior
**   Independent Variable = size of Yellow Pages ad**

```
Logit estimates                                 Number of firms =        40
                                                Wald chi2(1)    =      9.05
                                                Prob > chi2     =    0.0026
Log likelihood = -449.60778                     Pseudo R2       =    0.0287

                           (standard errors adjusted for clustering on comidno)
------------------------------------------------------------------------------
             |               Robust
        supq |     Coef.   Std. Err.      z    P>|z|     [95% Conf. Interval]
-------------+----------------------------------------------------------------
        yp96 | -.0224215    .007454    -3.01   0.003    -.0370311    -.007812
       _cons |  1.622553   .1432273    11.33   0.000     1.341832    1.903273
------------------------------------------------------------------------------
```

```
Regression 4:   Dependent Variable = size of yellow pages ad
                Independent Variable = value  (%superior/WCC price index)

  Source |      SS          df       MS              Number of firms =      36
---------+------------------------------            F( 1,    34) =      5.19
   Model | 1636.75634        1  1636.75634          Prob > F      =    0.0291
Residual | 10714.695        34   315.13809          R-squared     =    0.1325
---------+------------------------------            Adj R-squared =    0.1070
   Total | 12351.4514       35  352.898611          Root MSE      =    17.752


-------------------------------------------------------------------------------
    yp96 |    Coef.    Std. Err.        t     P>|t|     [95% Conf. Interval]
---------+---------------------------------------------------------------------
   value | -24.25008   10.64073     -2.279    0.029     -45.87465   -2.625506
   _cons |  33.12038    9.236143     3.586    0.001      14.35028   51.89048
-------------------------------------------------------------------------------


Regression 5:   Dependent Variable = number of employees
                Independent Variable = value (%superior/ WCC price index)

  Source |      SS          df       MS              Number of firms =      32
---------+------------------------------            F( 1,    30) =      1.20
   Model | 31.6064178        1  31.6064178          Prob > F      =    0.2822
Residual | 790.768582       30  26.3589527          R-squared     =    0.0384
---------+------------------------------            Adj R-squared =    0.0064
   Total | 822.375          31  26.5282258          Root MSE      =    5.1341


-------------------------------------------------------------------------------
 employ96 |    Coef.    Std. Err.       t     P>|t|     [95% Conf. Interval]
----------+--------------------------------------------------------------------
    value | -3.87234    3.536306     -1.095    0.282     -11.09444   3.349761
    _cons |  8.745292   3.044999      2.872    0.007       2.526574  14.96401
-------------------------------------------------------------------------------
```

Locksmiths
(1999)

The 1999 data set for Locksmiths is very small and lacks a Yellow Pages advertisement size variable. When this WCC rating was published, staff resources were no longer available to collect the relevant Yellow Pages data. In addition, WCC did not provide firm size data for Locksmiths. In Regression 1, the WCC price index is seen to be negatively correlated with the WCC quality index.

```
Regression 1:  Dependent Variable = %rating firm superior
               Independent variable = WCC price index

Logit estimates                              Number of firms =        25
                                             Prob > chi2     =    0.0031
Log likelihood = -280.46412                  Pseudo R2       =    0.0175

                             (standard errors adjusted for clustering on idno99)
-----------------------------------------------------------------------------
             |               Robust
        supq |     Coef.   Std. Err.      z    P>|z|     [95% Conf. Interval]
-------------+---------------------------------------------------------------
      price99 | -.0459347   .0155294    -2.96   0.003    -.0763717   -.0154977
       _cons |  5.978987   1.594268     3.75   0.000     2.854279    9.103695
-----------------------------------------------------------------------------
```

Major Appliance Repair
(1996)

This data set includes variables for price, firm size and size of Yellow Pages ad. As is evident in regressions 1-3, all of these variables are strongly and negatively associated with quality. Further analysis (not shown) revealed no correlation between the Yellow Pages variable and value as measured by quality adjusted for price. In Regression 4, the value variable is negatively correlated with firm size (as measured by number of employees). It should be noted that there is a high degree of direct intercorrelation among the independent variables in this data set. This can be seen in Regression 5, where none of the variables displays a significant coefficient when all are included in the same regression predicting quality.

```
Regression 1:  Dependent Variable = %rating firm adequate or superior
               Independent Variable = WCC price index

Logit estimates                              Number of firms =        46
                                             Wald chi2(1)    =     25.84
                                             Prob > chi2     =    0.0000
Log likelihood = -840.60736                  Pseudo R2       =    0.0411

                             (standard errors adjusted for clustering on comidno)
-----------------------------------------------------------------------------
             |               Robust
        supq |     Coef.   Std. Err.      z    P>|z|     [95% Conf. Interval]
-------------+---------------------------------------------------------------
      price96 | -.0473062   .0093066    -5.08   0.000    -.0655468   -.0290657
       _cons |  7.208831   1.048761     6.87   0.000     5.153297    9.264364
-----------------------------------------------------------------------------
```

Regression 2:   Dependent Variable = %rating firm adequate or superior
Independent Variable = number of employees

```
Logit estimates                                Number of firms =        54
                                               Wald chi2(1)     =     23.43
                                               Prob > chi2      =    0.0000
Log likelihood = -642.45782                    Pseudo R2        =    0.0513
```

                    (standard errors adjusted for clustering on comidno)

supq	Coef.	Robust Std. Err.	z	P>|z|	[95% Conf. Interval]	
employ96	-.0778501	.016082	-4.84	0.000	-.1093703	-.0463299
_cons	2.7201	.2109764	12.89	0.000	2.306594	3.133606

Regression 3:   Dependent Variable = %rating firm adequate or superior
Independent Variable = size of Yellow Pages ad

```
Logit estimates                                Number of firms =        35
                                               Wald chi2(1)     =      6.74
                                               Prob > chi2      =    0.0095
Log likelihood = -1005.0842                    Pseudo R2        =    0.0203
```

                    (standard errors adjusted for clustering on comidno)

supq	Coef.	Robust Std. Err.	z	P>|z|	[95% Conf. Interval]	
yp96	-.0253057	.0097507	-2.60	0.009	-.0444167	-.0061947
_cons	2.66959	.3206881	8.32	0.000	2.041053	3.298127

Regression 4:   Dependent Variable = number of employees
Independent Variable = value (quality/price)

```
regress  employ96   value
```

Source	SS	df	MS		Number of firms =	43
Model	111.030719	1	111.030719		F(1, 41) =	8.35
Residual	545.376258	41	13.3018599		Prob > F =	0.0061
					R-squared =	0.1691
					Adj R-squared =	0.1489
Total	656.406977	42	15.6287375		Root MSE =	3.6472

employ96	Coef.	Std. Err.	t	P>|t|	[95% Conf. Interval]	
value	-11.75401	4.068373	-2.889	0.006	-19.97026	-3.537767
_cons	14.47038	3.853586	3.755	0.001	6.687909	22.25286

```
Regression 5:   Dependent Variable = %rating firm adequate or superior
                Independent Variable = #employees, WCC price index, size of
                                       Yellow Pages ad

Logit estimates                                   Number of firms =          23
                                                  Wald chi2(3)    =        2.32
                                                  Prob > chi2     =      0.5093
Log likelihood = -214.21189                       Pseudo R2       =      0.0043

                              (standard errors adjusted for clustering on comidno)
------------------------------------------------------------------------------
             |               Robust
        supq |      Coef.   Std. Err.       z    P>|z|     [95% Conf. Interval]
-------------+----------------------------------------------------------------
     employ96 |   -.024605    .0360032    -0.68   0.494    -.0951699    .0459599
      price96 |  -.0134052    .0185372    -0.72   0.470    -.0497375    .0229271
         yp96 |    .008471    .0205447     0.41   0.680    -.0317959     .048738
        _cons |   4.198566    1.760559     2.38   0.017     .7479346    7.649198
------------------------------------------------------------------------------
```

Movers Local)
(1998)

This data set lacks information on firm size, but does include the Yellow Pages ad size variable. In addition, a dummy variable is used to identify firms that are agents for national moving company chains. This permits a test of the hypothesis that consumers can rely on a firm's status as an agent to signal higher quality. Two price variables are used in the regressions that follow. The first is the usual WCC price index, which in this sample was only available for 22 firms. The second is a firm's hourly wage rate for a crew of 3 during peak moving season, which was available for 26 firms.

Regressions 1 and 2 find no significant correlation between price and quality using either price measure. In Regression 3, Yellow Page ad size is not associated with quality. Further analysis (not shown) revealed that the Yellow Pages variable was not related to value as measured by the WCC quality score divided by the WCC price index or the hourly wage rate variable

Finally, Regression 4 shows that agents for national chains did not receive higher ratings than independent firms. The coefficient for the agent dummy is negative, although it does not achieve significance.

Regression 1:   Dependent Variable = %rating firm superior
              Independent Variable = WCC price index

Logit estimates   Number of firms =   22
                                                   Wald chi2(1)   =   0.00
                                                   Prob > chi2   =   0.9951
Log likelihood = -338.99512   Pseudo R2   =   0.0000

                          (standard errors adjusted for clustering on comidno)

             | Robust
        supq | Coef.   Std. Err.   z   P>|z| [95% Conf. Interval]
-------------+--
      price98 | .0001009   .0163045   0.01   0.995   -.0318552   .0320571
        _cons | 1.06614   1.616056   0.66   0.509   -2.101272   4.233553

Regression 2:   Dependent Variable = %rating firm superior
              Independent Variable = hourly wage rate, crew of 3

Logit estimates   Number of firms =   28
                                                   Wald chi2(1)   =   1.53
                                                   Prob > chi2   =   0.2163
Log likelihood = -397.5641   Pseudo R2   =   0.0100

                          (standard errors adjusted for clustering on comidno)

             | Robust
        supq | Coef.   Std. Err.   z   P>|z| [95% Conf. Interval]
-------------+--
      hour398 | .0199081   .0161001   1.24   0.216   -.0116475   .0514638
        _cons | -.8896816   1.643322   -0.54   0.588   -4.110533   2.33117

Regression 3:   Dependent Variable = %rating firm superior
              Independent Variable = size of Yellow Pages ad

Logit estimates   Number of firms =   28
                                                   Wald chi2(1)   =   0.11
                                                   Prob > chi2   =   0.7346
Log likelihood = -407.55673   Pseudo R2   =   0.0004

                          (standard errors adjusted for clustering on comidno)

             | Robust
        supq | Coef.   Std. Err.   z   P>|z| [95% Conf. Interval]
-------------+--
         yp98 | .0014154   .0041744   0.34   0.735   -.0067662   .009597
        _cons | .991965   .2576976   3.85   0.000   .486887   1.497043

```
Regression 4:   Dependent Variable = %rating firm superior
                Independent Variable = agent status (agent=1)

Logit estimates                                Number of firms =          30
                                               Wald chi2(1)    =        0.37
                                               Prob > chi2     =      0.5431
Log likelihood =  -425.2212                    Pseudo R2       =      0.0024

                              (standard errors adjusted for clustering on comidno)
--------------------------------------------------------------------------------
            |               Robust
       supq |    Coef.    Std. Err.      z     P>|z|     [95% Conf. Interval]
------------+-------------------------------------------------------------------
     agent98 | -.2566645    .42205    -0.61   0.543    -1.083867    .5705383
       _cons |  1.09089   .1886116     5.78   0.000     .7212183    1.460562
--------------------------------------------------------------------------------
```

Pest Control Firms
(1997)

The Pest Control data set contains information on firm size and Yellow Pages ad size, as well as two other variables that permit testing of signaling hypotheses. The first is a dummy variable identifying firms that are part of national chains. The second is a variable representing the length of the warranty period that firms offer for pest control work. This variable is used to test the hypothesis that consumers can rely on warranty length as a signal of the effectiveness of the initial treatment. WCC provides two price measures for pest control firms. One is the charge for a termite inspection with written report. The other is more complex and not easily adapted for use as a dependent variable.[1] All price regressions reported below employ the termite inspection charge.

Regression 1 shows a strong positive correlation between consumer satisfaction and price. In Regression 2, however, a similarly strong negative correlation surfaces between satisfaction and firm size and, in Regression 3, between satisfaction and size of Yellow Pages ad. In Regression 4, there is a significant negative relationship between the Yellow Pages variable and value (quality divided by price). The value variable also displays a significant negative coefficient when firm size is used as the dependent variable in Regression 5. Regression 6 reveals a strong negative

---

[1] This three-part measure consists of (1) a firm's estimated charge for the first treatment of a sample house, (2) the length of period during which the firm will perform a free follow-up treatment, and (3) the estimated charge for treatment after the free followup period. Various alternative specifications were constructed by compiling a composite index that weighted the initial treatment charge by the length of free followup period, and combined this with the charge after the followup period. All such composite measures were either negatively correlated with quality or uncorrelated. In any event, it is not clear which, if any, of the tested specifications is most appropriate, particularly since it is impossible to estimate expected total costs without firm-specific knowledge of the probability that followup treatments will be needed.

correlation between satisfaction and firm status as a member of a national chain. For the final signaling hypothesis, Regression 7 indicates that consumers cannot rely on the length of the warranty period for the initial treatment as a predictor of satisfaction. There is a significant negative correlation between these two variables.

All of the signaling variables are included as predictors of satisfaction in Regression 8. With the exception of size of Yellow Pages ad, all of the variables are significant and retain the same sign as displayed in the simple two way regression. Further analysis showed that the Yellow Pages variable is highly correlated with chain status (r=.52), and loses its explanatory power when both variables are used as predictors.

```
Regression 1:   Dependent Variable = %rating firm superior
                Independent Variable = termite inspection charge

Logit estimates                               Number of firms =          51
                                              Wald chi2(1)      =       16.96
                                              Prob > chi2       =      0.0000
Log likelihood = -1480.7173                   Pseudo R2         =      0.0173

                              (standard errors adjusted for clustering on comidno)
---------------------------------------------------------------------------------
             |              Robust
        supq |    Coef.    Std. Err.      z     P>|z|      [95% Conf. Interval]
-------------+-------------------------------------------------------------------
    chgter97 |  .0235317   .0057148     4.12    0.000      .0123309    .0347325
       _cons | -.8820023   .3129227    -2.82    0.005     -1.495319   -.2686851
---------------------------------------------------------------------------------


Regression 2:   Dependent Variable = %rating firm superior
                Independent Variable = number of employees

Logit estimates                               Number of firms =          55
                                              Wald chi2(1)      =       17.88
                                              Prob > chi2       =      0.0000
Log likelihood = -1585.6447                   Pseudo R2         =      0.0227

                              (standard errors adjusted for clustering on comidno)
---------------------------------------------------------------------------------
             |              Robust
        supq |    Coef.    Std. Err.      z     P>|z|      [95% Conf. Interval]
-------------+-------------------------------------------------------------------
     empls97 |  -.07324    .0173194    -4.23    0.000     -.1071855   -.0392946
       _cons |  .8631196   .2232701     3.87    0.000      .4255182    1.300721
---------------------------------------------------------------------------------
```

Regression 3:   Dependent Variable = %rating firm superior
**   Independent Variable = size of Yellow Pages ad**

```
Logit estimates                                   Number of firms =        51
                                                  Wald chi2(1)    =     12.23
                                                  Prob > chi2     =    0.0005
Log likelihood = -1512.4115                       Pseudo R2       =    0.0219
```

```
                          (standard errors adjusted for clustering on comidno)
-------------------------------------------------------------------------------
            |               Robust
      supq  |    Coef.     Std. Err.       z     P>|z|     [95% Conf. Interval]
------------+------------------------------------------------------------------
      yp97  |  -.0125807    .0035981    -3.50    0.000    -.0196328   -.0055286
     _cons  |   .792496     .2053677     3.86    0.000     .3899828    1.195009
-------------------------------------------------------------------------------
```

Regression 4:   Dependent Variable = size of Yellow Pages ad
**   Independent Variable = value (quality/price)**

```
    Source |      SS         df        MS              Number of firms =     48
-----------+----------------------------              F( 1,      46)  =    8.75
     Model |  5469.12685      1   5469.12685          Prob > F        =  0.0049
  Residual |  28742.3614     46   624.833944          R-squared       =  0.1599
-----------+----------------------------              Adj R-squared   =  0.1416
     Total |  34211.4883     47   727.904006          Root MSE        =  24.997
```

```
-------------------------------------------------------------------------------
      yp97 |    Coef.     Std. Err.       t     P>|t|      [95% Conf. Interval]
-----------+-------------------------------------------------------------------
     value | -22.58214    7.632881     -2.959   0.005     -37.94634   -7.217952
     _cons |  54.88138    10.37279      5.291   0.000      34.00205    75.76072
-------------------------------------------------------------------------------
```

Regression 5:   Dependent Variable = number of employees
**   Independent Variable = value (quality/price)**

```
    Source |      SS         df        MS              Number of firms =     51
-----------+----------------------------              F( 1,      49)  =    4.45
     Model |  66.4344209     1   66.4344209           Prob > F        =  0.0401
  Residual |  731.920183    49   14.9371466           R-squared       =  0.0832
-----------+----------------------------              Adj R-squared   =  0.0645
     Total |  798.354604    50   15.9670921           Root MSE        =  3.8649
```

```
-------------------------------------------------------------------------------
    empls97 |    Coef.    Std. Err.       t     P>|t|      [95% Conf. Interval]
-----------+-------------------------------------------------------------------
     value | -2.453904    1.163576     -2.109   0.040     -4.792198   -.1156102
     _cons |  8.672254    1.55833       5.565   0.000      5.540673    11.80383
-------------------------------------------------------------------------------
```

Regression 6:   Dependent Variable = %rating firm superior
Independent Variable = chain status   (chain=1)

Logit estimates

Number of firms =	57
Wald chi2(1) =	39.32
Prob > chi2 =	0.0000
Pseudo R2 =	0.0491

Log likelihood = -1607.7795

(standard errors adjusted for clustering on comidno)

supq	Coef.	Robust Std. Err.	z	P>|z|	[95% Conf. Interval]	
chain97	-1.078211	.1719506	-6.27	0.000	-1.415228	-.7411936
_cons	.721779	.1444339	5.00	0.000	.4386938	1.004864

Regression 7:   Dependent Variable = %superior, doing work properly
Independent Variable = length of warranty for initial treatment

Logit estimates

Number of firms =	42
Wald chi2(1) =	3.97
Prob > chi2 =	0.0462
Pseudo R2 =	0.0068

Log likelihood = -518.83793

(standard errors adjusted for clustering on comidno)

supq	Coef.	Robust Std. Err.	z	P>|z|	[95% Conf. Interval]	
period97	-.0015461	.0007756	-1.99	0.046	-.0030662	-.0000261
_cons	2.207526	.1784935	12.37	0.000	1.857685	2.557366

Regression 8:   Dependent Variable = %rating firm superior
Independent Variables = price index, firm size, size of Yellow
Pages ad, chain status

Logit estimates

Number of firms =	48
Wald chi2(4) =	80.19
Prob > chi2 =	0.0000
Pseudo R2 =	0.0705

Log likelihood = -1367.2647

(standard errors adjusted for clustering on comidno)

supq	Coef.	Robust Std. Err.	z	P>|z|	[95% Conf. Interval]	
chgter97	.0123134	.0065977	1.87	0.062	-.0006179	.0252447
empls97	-.057151	.0220553	-2.59	0.010	-.1003785	-.0139235
yp97	.0015786	.0034326	0.46	0.646	-.0051493	.0083064
chain97	-1.009009	.2715573	-3.72	0.000	-1.541252	-.4767667
_cons	.453565	.4369342	1.04	0.299	-.4028103	1.30994

Plumbers
(1995)

The 1995 data set for Plumbers contains variables for size of firm and Yellow Pages ad. The dependent variable, however, is the less sensitive overall satisfaction measure that combines superior and adequate ratings. A dummy variable was also constructed to identify members of a national chain (of which there was only one.) Analysis (not shown) revealed that this variable was unrelated to consumer satisfaction or to any of the other independent variables.

Regression 1 shows a strong negative correlation between price and quality. Regression 2 reveals a similarly strong negative relationship between quality and firm size. In Regression 3, there is an even more systematic negative relationship between size of Yellow Pages ad and quality. Regression 4 shows that Yellow Pages ad size cannot be used to identify firms providing particularly good value in terms of price-adjusted quality. This reflects a positive correlation between the Yellow Pages variable and price (r=.390). Value is also negatively correlated with firm size, as shown in Regression 5. Finally, Regression 6 reveals that the Yellow Pages variable demonstrates the greatest predictive power in a regression that employs all of the independent variables. This suggests that Yellow Pages ad size is not merely functioning as a proxy for price or firm size in this data set.

```
Regression 1:  Dependent Variable = %rating firm superior or adequate
               Independent Variable = WCC price index

Logit estimates                              Number of firms =        134
                                             Wald chi2(1)    =       7.37
                                             Prob > chi2     =     0.0066
Log likelihood = -1657.9036                  Pseudo R2       =     0.0083

                          (standard errors adjusted for clustering on comidno)
------------------------------------------------------------------------------
             |               Robust
      supq |      Coef.   Std. Err.       z    P>|z|     [95% Conf. Interval]
-------------+----------------------------------------------------------------
   price95 |  -.0229292    .0084459    -2.71   0.007    -.0394828    -.0063755
      _cons |   4.895038    .8762987     5.59   0.000     3.177524     6.612551
------------------------------------------------------------------------------
```

Regression 2: Dependent Variable = %rating firm superior or adequate
Independent Variable = number of employees

Logit estimates

```
                                        Number of firms  =        137
                                        Wald chi2(1)     =       6.24
                                        Prob > chi2      =     0.0125
Log likelihood = -1758.2104             Pseudo R2        =     0.0078
```

(standard errors adjusted for clustering on comidno)

```
----------------------------------------------------------------------
             |               Robust
        supq |     Coef.   Std. Err.       z     P>|z|    [95% Conf. Interval]
-------------+--------------------------------------------------------------
    employ95 | -.0140669   .0056328    -2.50    0.013   -.0251069   -.0030269
       _cons |  2.617006   .1228796    21.30    0.000    2.376167    2.857846
----------------------------------------------------------------------
```

Regression 3: Dependent Variable = %rating firm superior or adequate
Independent Variable = size of Yellow Pages ad

Logit estimates

```
                                        Number of firms  =        117
                                        Wald chi2(1)     =      13.19
                                        Prob > chi2      =     0.0003
Log likelihood = -1558.1123             Pseudo R2        =     0.0391
```

(standard errors adjusted for clustering on comidno)

```
----------------------------------------------------------------------
             |               Robust
        supq |     Coef.   Std. Err.       z     P>|z|    [95% Conf. Interval]
-------------+--------------------------------------------------------------
        yp95 | -.0187058   .0051502    -3.63    0.000      -.0288   -.0086117
       _cons |  2.882208   .1253447    22.99    0.000    2.636536    3.127879
----------------------------------------------------------------------
```

Regression 4: Dependent Variable = size of Yellow Pages ad
Independent Variable = Value (quality/price)

```
      Source |       SS       df       MS              Number of firms  =    113
-------------+------------------------------            F(  1,   111)   =   35.18
       Model | 16631.9631      1   16631.9631           Prob > F         = 0.0000
    Residual | 52472.1909    111   472.72244            R-squared        = 0.2407
-------------+------------------------------            Adj R-squared    = 0.2338
       Total | 69104.154     112   617.001375           Root MSE         = 21.742
```

```
----------------------------------------------------------------------
        yp95 |     Coef.   Std. Err.       t     P>|t|    [95% Conf. Interval]
-------------+--------------------------------------------------------------
       value |  -84.0762   14.17439    -5.932    0.000   -112.1637   -55.9887
       _cons |  93.41068   12.97204     7.201    0.000    67.70572   119.1156
----------------------------------------------------------------------
```

Regression 5: Dependent Variable = number of employees
Independent Variable = value (quality/price)

Source	SS	df	MS			
Model	2268.99974	1	2268.99974	Number of firms =		133
Residual	25955.7296	131	198.13534	F(1, 131) =		11.45
				Prob > F =		0.0009
				R-squared =		0.0804
				Adj R-squared =		0.0734
Total	28224.7293	132	213.823707	Root MSE =		14.076

employ95	Coef.	Std. Err.	t	P>|t|	[95% Conf. Interval]	
value	-28.16574	8.323095	-3.384	0.001	-44.6308	-11.70067
_cons	33.88606	7.774728	4.358	0.000	18.50579	49.26632

Regression 6: Dependent Variable = %rating firm superior or adequate
Independent Variable = WCC price index, size of Yellow Pages
ad, number of employees

Logit estimates

Number of firms =	112
Wald chi2(3) =	25.11
Prob > chi2 =	0.0000
Pseudo R2 =	0.0267

Log likelihood = -1469.8097

(standard errors adjusted for clustering on comidno)

supq	Coef.	Robust Std. Err.	z	P>|z|	[95% Conf. Interval]	
price95	-.0129418	.0094567	-1.37	0.171	-.0314765	.0055929
yp95	-.0136778	.0045599	-3.00	0.003	-.022615	-.0047407
employ95	-.0037818	.0038631	-0.98	0.328	-.0113534	.0037897
_cons	4.179633	.9420912	4.44	0.000	2.333168	6.026098

Restaurants
(1998)

This very large data set contains consumer evaluations of 672 restaurants in the Washington D.C. area. Respondents were asked to base their ratings on a scale of 0 through 100, and to rate a restaurant on quality of food, quality of service, and on value. Thus, for this one industry, the quality ratings may not be confounded to any extent with the price ratings, since consumers were specifically asked to provide a separate rating for price-adjusted quality. WCC assigned restaurants to one of five price categories. Although the quality variable is truncated at both ends, the ratings were fairly evenly distributed and did not bunch at the upper truncation point (100). For these reasons, the regressions were run in ordinary least squares format.

Price and food quality are very highly correlated in Regression 1. Note that the coefficients for the four dummy variables (with category 1 the eliminated variable) increase monotonically, showing that quality increases with each increment in the price grouping. The same pattern emerges for quality of service in Regression 2, with even higher significance levels for all of the coefficients. WCC did not collect firm size data for restaurants, and Yellow Pages ad size data were not collected due to resource constraints and the perceived low probability that such a variable would be correlated with quality in this industry.

Regression 1: Dependent Variable = food quality (0-100)
**   Independent Variable = price category**

```
Regression with robust standard errors          Number of firms =   672
                                                F(  4,    671) =   25.84
                                                Prob > F       =  0.0000
                                                R-squared      =  0.1608
Number of clusters (idno98) = 672               Root MSE       =  5.4838

----------------------------------------------------------------------------
           |              Robust
   food98  |     Coef.   Std. Err.       t     P>|t|     [95% Conf. Interval]
---------+------------------------------------------------------------------
    p298  |  2.717179   .6798711      3.997   0.000     1.382249     4.05211
    p398  |  4.282356   .7127837      6.008   0.000     2.882801    5.681911
    p498  |  7.125349   .8785988      8.110   0.000     5.400215    8.850483
    p598  |  10.91182   1.548333      7.047   0.000     7.871658    13.95198
    cons  |     71.77   .6033904    118.945   0.000     70.58524    72.95476
----------------------------------------------------------------------------
```


Regression 2: Dependent Variable = service quality (0-100)
**   Independent Variable = price category**

```
Regression with robust standard errors          Number of firms =   672
                                                F(  4,    671) =   37.01
                                                Prob > F       =  0.0000
                                                R-squared      =  0.2062
Number of clusters (idno98) = 672               Root MSE       =  5.1995

----------------------------------------------------------------------------
           |              Robust
  servic98 |     Coef.   Std. Err.       t     P>|t|     [95% Conf. Interval]
---------+------------------------------------------------------------------
    p298  |   3.40044   .5966455      5.699   0.000     2.228923    4.571956
    p398  |  5.117487   .6263974      8.170   0.000     3.887552    6.347422
    p498  |  8.467907   .8089955     10.467   0.000      6.87944    10.05637
    p598  |  11.02182   1.557838      7.075   0.000     7.962995    14.08064
    cons  |     68.16    .513327    132.781   0.000     67.15208    69.16792
----------------------------------------------------------------------------
```

Shoe Repair
(1995)

The Shoe Repair data set for 1995 contains price and quality information for 95 firms. Although WCC did not collect information on firm size, the data set does contain a Yellow Pages ad size variable. Regression 1 shows a negative but not quite significant negative correlation between price and quality. In Regression 2, the size of a firm's Yellow Pages ad is positively associated with quality. Further analysis (not shown) revealed no association between the Yellow Pages variable and value as measured by the price-adjusted WCC quality rating.

```
Regression 1:  Dependent Variable = %percent rating firm superior
               Independent Variable = WCC price index

Logit estimates                              Number of firms =        95
                                             Wald chi2(1)    =      2.28
                                             Prob > chi2     =    0.1310
Log likelihood = -1284.0179                  Pseudo R2       =    0.0019

                          (standard errors adjusted for clustering on comidno)
------------------------------------------------------------------------------
             |               Robust
        supq |     Coef.   Std. Err.      z    P>|z|     [95% Conf. Interval]
-------------+----------------------------------------------------------------
      price95 | -.0098966   .0065534   -1.51   0.131    -.0227411    .002948
        _cons |  2.555293   .6473709    3.95   0.000     1.286469   3.824116
------------------------------------------------------------------------------


Regression 2:  Dependent Variable = %rating firm superior
               Independent Variable = size of Yellow Pages ad

Logit estimates                              Number of firms =        77
                                             Wald chi2(1)    =      8.83
                                             Prob > chi2     =    0.0030
Log likelihood = -1135.0913                  Pseudo R2       =    0.0084

                          (standard errors adjusted for clustering on comidno)
------------------------------------------------------------------------------
             |               Robust
        supq |     Coef.   Std. Err.      z    P>|z|     [95% Conf. Interval]
-------------+----------------------------------------------------------------
        yp95 |  .1727471   .0581234    2.97   0.003     .0588274   .2866668
        _cons |  1.401833   .1263968   11.09   0.000       1.1541   1.649566
------------------------------------------------------------------------------
```

Supermarkets
(2001)

The Supermarkets data set for 2001 includes only 8 firms, but over 10,000 respondents provided ratings based on experiences at dozens of individual stores. Regression 1 shows a very strong positive correlation between price and quality in this industry.

```
Regression 1:   Dependent Variable = % rating store superior
                Independent Variable = WCC price index

Logit estimates                                 Number of chains =           8
                                                Wald chi2(1)     =      116.89
                                                Prob > chi2      =      0.0000
Log likelihood = -6870.3591                     Pseudo R2        =      0.0337

                             (standard errors adjusted for clustering on idno)
------------------------------------------------------------------------------
             |               Robust
       supq  |    Coef.    Std. Err.      z     P>|z|     [95% Conf. Interval]
-------------+----------------------------------------------------------------
      price  |  .0413359   .0038233     10.81   0.000    .0338424     .0488294
      _cons  | -4.419366   .4628962     -9.55   0.000   -5.326626    -3.512106
------------------------------------------------------------------------------
```

TV Repair
(1989)

The 1989 ratings for TV Repair were the last to include a price index for actual repairs. The 1991 ratings provide information only on a firm's charge for a repair estimate. Neither firm size nor contemporaneous Yellow Pages ad size data could be obtained for the firms in the 1989 data set. Regression 1 shows a negative but insignificant correlation between price and the percentage of respondents rating a firm superior or adequate in overall quality.

```
Regression 1:   Dependent Variable = %rating firm superior or adequate

Logit estimates                                 Number of firms  =          36
                                                Wald chi2(1)     =        1.04
                                                Prob > chi2      =      0.3072
Log likelihood = -372.66854                     Pseudo R2        =      0.0055

                             (standard errors adjusted for clustering on idno)
------------------------------------------------------------------------------
             |               Robust
       supq  |    Coef.    Std. Err.      z     P>|z|     [95% Conf. Interval]
-------------+----------------------------------------------------------------
      price  | -.0089139   .0087299     -1.02   0.307   -.0260241     .0081964
      _cons  |  3.061545   .9877203      3.10   0.002    1.125649     4.997442
------------------------------------------------------------------------------
```

Tree Experts
(1999)

The 1999 data set for Tree Experts is limited to information on price and quality. WCC could not provide firm size data, and resources were no longer available to collect Yellow Pages ad size data. Regression 1 shows no significant correlation between price and quality.

```
Regression 1:  Dependent Variable = %rating firm superior
               Independent Variable = WCC price index

Logit estimates                              Number of firms =          29
                                             Wald chi2(1)    =        0.70
                                             Prob > chi2     =      0.4029`
Log likelihood = -505.6894                   Pseudo R2       =      0.0031

                          (standard errors adjusted for clustering on idno99)
------------------------------------------------------------------------------
             |               Robust
        supq |     Coef.   Std. Err.      z    P>|z|     [95% Conf. Interval]
-------------+----------------------------------------------------------------
     price99 |   .0069715    .008334    0.84   0.403    -.0093627    .0233058
       _cons |   .6667981   .8065977    0.83   0.408    -.9141043    2.247701
------------------------------------------------------------------------------
```

Watch Repair
(1996)

The 1996 data set for Watch Repair contains information on Yellow Pages ad size, but not firm size. In Regression 1, The WCC quality ratings and the WCC price index are uncorrelated. Similarly, in Regression 2, there is no significant relationship between quality and size of Yellow Pages ad. Further analysis (not shown) failed to find any significant correlation between the Yellow Pages variable and price or value (quality divided by price).

```
Regression 1:  Dependent Variable = %rating firm superior
               Independent Variable = WCC price index

Logit estimates                              Number of firms =          41
                                             Wald chi2(1)    =        0.12
                                             Prob > chi2     =      0.7321
Log likelihood = -622.39017                  Pseudo R2       =      0.0002

                          (standard errors adjusted for clustering on idno96)
------------------------------------------------------------------------------
             |               Robust
        supq |     Coef.   Std. Err.      z    P>|z|     [95% Conf. Interval]
-------------+----------------------------------------------------------------
     price96 |  -.0018618   .0054376   -0.34   0.732    -.0125193    .0087958
       _cons |   1.371141   .5230825    2.62   0.009     .3459186    2.396364
------------------------------------------------------------------------------
```

Regression 2: Dependent Variable = %rating firm superior
Independent Variable = size of Yellow Pages ad

```
Logit estimates                                 Number of obs   =        37
                                                Wald chi2(1)    =      0.01
                                                Prob > chi2     =    0.9065
Log likelihood = -707.40833                     Pseudo R2       =    0.0000
```

(standard errors adjusted for clustering on idno96)

supq	Coef.	Robust Std. Err.	z	P>|z|	[95% Conf. Interval]	
yp96	-.0093096	.0792308	-0.12	0.906	-.1645991	.1459799
_cons	1.191147	.1316236	9.05	0.000	.933169	1.449124